A Roomful of Elephants

A Roomful of Elephants

My First 80 Years in the Church

PATRICK FORBES

BAUHAN PUBLISHING
PETERBOROUGH · NEW HAMPSHIRE
2021

A CIP catalogue for this book is available from the British Library
BNB GBC170226; System number: 020182344

Library of Congress Cataloging-in-Publication Data
Names: Forbes, Patrick, 1938-author.
Title: A roomful of elephants : my first 80 years in the church / Patrick Forbes.
Description: First. | Peterborough, New Hampshire : Bauhan Publishing, 2021.
Identifiers: LCCN 2021012183 | ISBN 9780872333420 |
ISBN 9780872333437 (ebook)
Subjects: LCSH: Forbes, Patrick, 1938- | Church of England—Clergy—
Biography.
Classification: LCC BX5199.F59 A3 2021 | DDC 283.092 [B—dc23
LC record available at https://lccn.loc.gov/2021012183

Book design by Sarah Bauhan.
Cover design by Alison Gates and Henry James.
Cover painting by Mary Young.
Author photograph by Peter Hoskins Photography.

BAUHAN
PUBLISHING LLC
PO BOX 117 PETERBOROUGH NEW HAMPSHIRE 03458
603-567-4430
WWW.BAUHANPUBLISHING.COM

UK Distribution

CASEMATE | uk
The Old Music Hall,
106-108 Cowley Rd.,
Oxford, OX4 1JE
WWW.CASEMATEPUBLISHERS.CO.UK

Printed in the United Kingdom

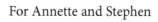

For Annette and Stephen

CONTENTS

Roly Bain and me

A few years ago, when I was asked to write an article on what I would do if I were the Archbishop of Canterbury, one of my determinations was to engage a Fool at Lambeth Palace. This Fool would attend meetings and, without speaking or uttering a sound, react to the comments and decisions of the assembled throng. He would also lurk idly in and around the various State Rooms at important receptions and scamper up and down the grand staircase when I was receiving eminent visitors. I felt such a colleague would help to keep me and my guests grounded, should we ever start to drift off towards the stratosphere of serious ecclesiastical pomposity. The man I had in mind for the job was, of course, Patrick Forbes.

Playing the fool is something that Patrick actually does, or certainly did, for many years, after co-founding a troupe of clowns called the Holy Fools in 1982 with the Reverend Roly Bain, a fellow priest and professional clown, and others. The Holy Fools were invited to perform in prisons and hospitals and at all kinds of conferences, and also to take services while in their clown personas. They even occasionally threw custard pies in the faces of some Anglican bishops, who, I am told, took such antics in extremely good grace.

Once during a radio interview, Patrick explained that 'There are ways of sharing the gospel which are not necessarily solemn and Bible-thumping. There may be gentler, quieter, and sometimes outrageously funny ways of sharing the Good News of Jesus with other people.'

Anyone who knows Patrick will know that having him around can introduce a rollercoaster ride of the unexpected, veering from the inevitably temporarily and deceptively sedate to the hilarious and absurd. Patrick's seagull impersonations are legendary, and I have found that his trombone playing alone is quite enough to reduce most people to tears. But anyone who mistakenly thinks Patrick is just a fool, holy or otherwise, misses the point of what makes Patrick tick, for I have rarely met someone so passionate about communicating the liberating truth of the gospel to a world desperate for some real Good News.

Patrick's clowning may bring delight to others, but I have learned over the forty years we have been friends that it is also Patrick's way of dealing with the pain, injustices, and sometimes just the maddening frustrations of life. With humour, Patrick transmutes the tragic, illogical, and unfair into lighter, less daunting fragments that can be acknowledged and then released and allowed to dance away on the breezes of change, leaving hearts and minds intact, steadied and comforted. I can testify to times when I have been very low, when Patrick has ministered to me with the kindness and wisdom of someone who has also suffered and who has nevertheless found a loving, compassionate God in the midst of that suffering.

In this, his latest offering, Patrick sketches out the influences on his own life, what has mattered to him and what remains dear and precious. He dares to take on the shams, inconsistencies, and outright hypocrisies of the church he loves and to which he has given over half a century of creative, unstinting, and sacrificial service.

If you only have time to read a bit of this book, then read the last chapter where Patrick lets loose with a holy and righteous rant, naming certain elephants that have been lumbering around the Church of England for far too long, damaging fragile shoots and trampling loyalty and hope. But Patrick doesn't just rant: he offers a vision of how things could be better, a vision honed from his immensely varied and remarkable ministry. In the end, Patrick is a prophet, and the church would do well to take him seriously, and not be thrown by the fact that sometimes he just feels the need to preach with a plastic bucket over his head.

Christina Rees

Why on earth?

When thinking about a title for this book, my first thought was *The Bumper Book of Anglican Fun (abridged)*. Reflecting on what I wanted to write, it later occurred to me that *A Roomful of Elephants* might be more appropriate. For the Church of England is blessed or cursed with a roomful of elephants of differing ages and sizes, which threaten to burst the walls of the room in which they stand, so numerous are they, and so likely to grow and reproduce. And our Church, whatever else it is known for, is rarely the go-to place for fun – more's the pity, though from time to time I have tried to do something about that. I am, after all, the only pantomime horse to have been blessed by the Archbishop of Canterbury.

I like elephants. Our house is stuffed with pictures, models of elephants. Friends even bought us a concrete elephant for our golden wedding anniversary. Elmer the Elephant stands under an old apple tree in the garden. Elephants in the room, though, are a distraction, a menace when they are ignored. Unrecognised they can destroy an organisation.

Elephants abound within the Church of England. What is the Church for? Why do we have bishops and archdeacons? How are clergy and their leaders chosen, trained, rewarded? Do we need dioceses or the general synod? What about all the land the Church owns? Is the Church of England a service agency or a society for the preservation of immensely expensive and sometimes very ugly and inappropriate church buildings? Love them or hate them, buildings are the glories and the horrors of the Church of England. Sixteen thousand churches and 42 cathedrals cry out to be used, restored, embellished, cared for, or pulled down. There are assumptions that someone knows the answer and it might be best not to ask the questions for fear of seeming ignorant, subversive, or downright mischievous. But the more complicated the world becomes, the more urgent is the need for a basic and shared understanding of the point and purpose of organisations which hope to survive and grow.

So, my best friend Chris Rees asked, who is this book for? A good question, I thought. The book is for anyone who likes reading biographies. It is for people hovering or tiptoeing anywhere near a church, wondering whether they should risk going in, or continuing to belong to one more of our crumbling institutions.

If pushed, I would go on to say that storytelling holds the key to understanding who we are, where we might be going, and who or what might help us on the journey. What else are the Bible, the gospels, church history but stories that matter? Somebody once told me I was a boundary rider, someone who travels along the edge, who may see the value of the centre holding but is not overly impressed by the energies spent on maintaining something which may be incapable of reform or rebuilding. And the more I thought about teetering on the edge, the more it made sense, for that is where growth, meeting, movement, and change seem to be. So, my story may seem a bit edgy. I hope so.

The Church of England has been a sort of home to me, a kind of friend to me. One of its strengths is its breadth of membership, its spectrum of faith and practice. For that I am both amazed and grateful. Amazed because in so much of today's world, there are moves to narrow, to close down, to shut off possibilities. And grateful because I guess I am not the easiest of priests. Ideas, some would say mad ideas, are what excite me and scare me in equal measure. Yet the Church has taken me in, at times encouraged me to push ahead in edgy areas like faith and foolishness, broadcasting, and community development.

And a constant along the way has been the presence of pachyderms, elephants in the building, rumblings in the room, hints and near uncertainties of questions unanswered, unacknowledged, ignored. As a sort of sailor, I have nightmares about cargo shifting to the point where the vessel loses stability, the rats have left, and the master orders the boats swung out and the life rafts launched.

Where are the elephants in this book? Trust me, you may find them hard to miss.

CHAPTER 1

Beginnings

I might not have happened. I was born over eighty years ago in Weston-super-Mare in Somerset. They tell me that I was induced early so that my journalist mother could meet a deadline. My mother, Evelyn Forbes, told me once that her doctor had advised against the pregnancy as she would be thirty-nine when I was born in November 1938. On good days, she said, she was glad she hadn't taken the advice. 'On bad days. . . .' she would let the sentence hang in the air, leaving me to work it out for myself.

I was the youngest of four children. In 1926 my brother Ian Robert Patrick was born in India where my parents settled after their marriage in 1925. My sister Elizabeth Anne was born in 1933. The family returned to England the following year on medical advice. It was thought that Liz wouldn't survive the Indian climate. William Michael was born in 1934 in Weston-super-Mare.

Within a year of my birth the world was at war. I remember staying with my great-uncle John, who was a priest at Much Dewchurch in Herefordshire and a canon of Hereford Cathedral. He was unmarried and had a housekeeper, Mrs Taylor, and a gardener/chauffeur, Myned Griffin. Great-uncle John, or the Bonkler Man as we called him, a corruption of the French L'Oncle Jean, walked with a pronounced limp and I remember us children imitating his strange walk. If I were very good, I would be allowed to sit on his knee in his tip of a study and watch him as he lit his pipe. He had a great beard, and a student of gastronomy might trace what he had been recently eating. He always had porridge for breakfast. Mrs Taylor made him and us a different kind of milk pudding every day for lunch. I cannot face milk puddings.

I don't remember much about church until we moved to Burford, where we spent the war in a beautiful house called The Barn House. It was owned by my mother's great friend Katharine Briggs, whom she had met at school in Perthshire. Katharine was a world authority on folklore and fairy tales.

There are stories of misdemeanours in the Church of St John the Baptist, Burford. During a sermon by the vicar the Reverend Fairfax Scott Tucker, whom I remember as being quite a small, spherical priest, a squeaky voice – mine I am told – was heard from near the back of the church: 'I know where he got that. It was from *Lift Up Your Hearts!*' I suspect this is the earliest evidence of any interest in preaching and religious broadcasting. On another occasion, when the collecting plate came around, I emptied a paper bag full of nails into it. They made a splendid noise. I remember nothing of the Sunday School other than the sticky stamps we were given for attending. After church and Sunday School, oh joy – collecting a Beano or Dandy from the newsstand by the churchyard wall. No church, no comic. I do remember a tall, thin curate called Mr Rogers who turned up one day at the house and said, 'The vicar told me to call.'

After the war, we returned to London when it was safe to do so. My mother had a house in Chester Row, Number 21. I can still remember the rag-and-bone man with his horse and cart and his cries of 'any old rags and lumber.' Removals were still handled in giant covered carts pulled by horses. Some London buses had their stairs on the outside at the back of the bus. Coal for the fire was shot through a hole in the pavement into the coal store beneath the road.

I was sent to Eaton House School. The headmaster, Mr G. B. C. Lemon, beat me with the wing nut-end of a board compass, very painful it was too. I cannot remember for what offence that beating was applied. But my earliest nightmare came to me while I was at the school. I dreamed that I had stabbed a boy called Buster Tomlinson with an indelible pencil. I don't think I ever committed such a crime. Maybe it was something I thought a good idea at the time. Apart from one or two motoring offences, I don't think I have a criminal record, or if I have no-one has told me about it . . . yet.

Post-war London was a vast adventure playground. Underneath Eaton Square, along from the school, we discovered air raid shelters, a rat run of dark rooms and corridors, a paradise for young adventurers. Bomb sites were all around. There was a branch of the grocer Oakeshotts opposite the one pub in the street, The Duke of Wellington, on the corner of Eaton Terrace. One of my earliest photographs was of Martha Jacobsen, who looked after us, standing on the roof of 21 Chester Row, and another was of a shop girl from Oakeshotts standing outside the shop. Butter and cheese and bacon were sliced and weighed; sugar was sold in blue paper bags tied with string. There was a delightful absence of the stupid array of choices now on offer in shops and supermarkets. There was just butter, there was just cheese, just bacon. Someone said the other day that there are over a hundred different kinds of bread on offer in Tesco. What could possibly be good about that?

In 1947 I was sent to boarding school in Eastbourne. In later years my mother told me it was because she couldn't stand having me at home. I think the last straw may have been her coming home from work one evening to find that I and my horrid little friends had been playing hide-and-seek and she discovered one or more of us under her bed when she was changing out of her office clothes into something a little looser, like a housecoat.

There was a school train from Victoria Station to Eastbourne. On this train I met my oldest friend, Anthony Hawkins, also on his way to St Bede's. He recently celebrated his eightieth birthday in December, a month after mine. For some reason I called him Moke. We both wore glasses, and he was much more into sport than I ever was or shall be. His family lived in Chislehurst, within cycling distance of Victoria where we lived.

The school was my introduction to drama. One year we performed a cut-down version of *Twelfth Night*. I played Feste the clown to Anthony Hawkins' Malvolio. It was great fun and may have been my unwitting introduction to the business of clowns and clowning. I can still remember a boy dressed as a woman in some other production. Her one line was 'Words fail me!' That's the sort of part my memory can manage. I fear it may be a sad fact of my life that my head is filled with all kinds of hugely useless information – the gross registered tonnage of a Royal Mail Ship on which I later worked – 8,617.23 tons; the average thickness of electrical transformer laminations, though I think I may have just forgotten that precise number. Things that really matter find very little room in what is a memory crowded with comic verses, words of songs, and not a bad geography of London. I believe my whole education could be summed up this way: 'He retained enough information to pass most of his examinations, after which all that he had learned leaked away from his memory.' Is that a terrible fault? I don't think so. Memory shortage has encouraged my imagination, my interest in improvisation.

My brother Mike joined the school while it was still evacuated to Oxford. Our time in Eastbourne overlapped by three terms before he won a scholarship to the Royal Naval College, Dartmouth, so for a while we were Forbes 1 and Forbes 2.

The years passed at St Bede's, and half-terms came and went, usually without much sight of my parents. I learned one day that I was to be entered for an examination at Westminster School, called the Challenge. My mother, clearly reconciled to having me live at home during term time, had discovered that if I did tolerably well in this exam, I would be allowed to join Westminster without having had my name put down at my birth and without having to pay an entrance fee.

'You won't get an exhibition,' said the St Bede's chaplain, the Reverend Mr Copsey. 'You're not offering Greek,' he added. Not too reassured and thoroughly un-briefed about the school, I travelled to London and spent hours and hours panicking my way through any number of examination papers in the huge cold school hall at Westminster. At some point I was formally interviewed by some ten or so black-gowned members of staff in a large oak-panelled room called the Busby Library.

'What sport do you play?' asked one of these be-gowned gentlemen. 'Rugby,' I answered quick as a flash. There was a silence. The teachers looked at one another, clearly shocked. No-one had told me that Westminster along with, I think, Charterhouse, had invented soccer. One of the teachers said, 'What about water?' I must have looked both lost and baffled. 'Water, water, rowing,' one of them added, probably despairing of me. 'I've never rowed,' I said.

I must have got something right as I joined Westminster School in 1952. Maybe they were short of takers that autumn. I discovered that the fees at St Bede's for a boarder were some £65 a term, which were about equivalent to a day-boy's term fees at Westminster.

By then, we were living in Chester Street, in a flat rented to us by the Honourable Dowager Marchioness Townshend of Raynham. You would need a very wide envelope just to get her name and title on the paper. She was a kindly old lady with a past that may have bordered on the lively. She took me every year to a play of an improving nature at the Westminster Theatre which I later discovered was owned or run by something called Moral Rearmament. Maybe she hoped to influence me with such plays. I have absolutely no recollection of the plays, but I do remember the mushrooms on toast at a Lyons teashop near Victoria Station which formed part of the treat. Lady Townshend made it into the newspaper once a year throwing a Christmas party for Westminster City Council dustmen. Good for her!

Our local parish church was St Michael's, Chester Square. We sometimes went to evensong there and sat in the gallery at the west end of the church. From there we got a good view of the vicar Canon Gillingham's bald head as he stood in the pulpit under a fringed lamp. We often saw the old Queen Mother, Queen Mary, sitting in the front row on the left. Canon Gillingham was a chaplain to King George. Just for fun a few years ago I called at an estate agent in Elizabeth Street and asked how much it would cost to buy a house in Chester Row, 'about one million, seven hundred and fifty thousand pounds,' I was told. 'Don't get too excited,' I remarked as I left.

I enjoyed my four years at Westminster School. I don't think I was ever beaten there. Maybe all the beatings before I arrived had some effect after all. I did once have a run-in with the art master, Mr Spaull. There was a rhyme about him. 'Mr Spaull, when asked at all what was his line, said, "Byzantine."' It all blew up one lunch time in College Hall. Mr Spaull sat at the head of the table, made from very thick oak said to be from one of the wrecks of the Spanish Armada. He complained to us that nobody had passed him any vegetables. For the life of me I cannot remember if he had asked for the vegetables. Anyway, in response I made a point of passing him every dish of vegetables I could see. Mr Spaull complained to my housemaster Stephen Lushington who called me to see him and said I stood accused of dumb insolence. He said I should apologize to Mr Spaull, which I dutifully did. I had discovered the meaning and danger of dumb insolence. O God, another trait.

Religion played a considerable part in school life at Westminster. We had Latin Prayers on Monday and Wednesday afternoons at 3.15. This was probably a rule laid down in the time of Queen Elizabeth I. As the time for Latin Prayers drew near, there would be a knock at the classroom door and a junior Queen's Scholar would poke his face around the door and utter a squeaky Latin warning which sounded like 'Instat Sesquitertia' and then go on his way.

Every weekday morning, we assembled in Westminster Abbey for morning prayers. Our house, Wren's, was placed among the dead bards and sages in the south transept's Poets' Corner. Every three years there was an appallingly long service, all in Latin, the 'Commendatio Benefactorum,' the Commemoration of Benefactors, in Westminster Abbey. 'Send your money to the Bursar and be mentioned at Commem.,' was one musical saw not included in the three-hour service. I'm almost certain that the bursar's surname was St-John Carruthers. I was at Westminster for four years but only remember enduring one of these dreadful services. Perhaps I threw a tactical sick note.

My parents said I should be prepared for confirmation. I didn't even know what confirmation was or neglected to ask. I endured several after school confirmation sessions with the school chaplain. Alas, I found the view outside the classroom much more interesting than what was being discussed or dictated in the room. I was confirmed in St Margaret's Church as Westminster Abbey was being prepared for the Queen's coronation in June 1953. I can't remember much about either the course or the service itself. Maybe we were all warned to go easy with Brylcreem for fear of oiling the bishop's hands. All this religion left me cold. I think, looking back, that the emphasis was on religion, doing things in church, and less on faith and belief. There was no buzz, no excitement, and little if any joy.

My local parish church was St Peter's Church, Eaton Square. I recall that it was Anglo-Catholic, high church, smells and bells, and I did not feel either welcome or at home there. I went a few times on my own and then we moved from Chester Street to 78 Carlisle Mansions, Carlisle Place just off Victoria Street. The parish church serving that street was St Stephen's Church, Rochester Row. This was a more welcoming, down-to-earth church. I remember a man standing outside the church on Sundays. Dressed in full morning coat and striped trousers, he looked visitors up and down in order, I imagine, to decide whether we should be allowed in. It was a church with many curates, one of whom was Eric James whom I came to know years later when he was Canon Missioner of St Albans Diocese. The vicar was George Reindorp who later became Bishop of Guildford.

I stayed one more year at Westminster and added the study of German to my small list of studies. Annoyingly one of my fellow students by the name of Mark Overstall passed his German O level while I did not. Then I discovered he had spent some six weeks the previous summer staying with a German family. Throughout my time at Westminster I was in the same form as Corin Redgrave, and whenever a school play was being cast, he would get the plum parts with hundreds of lines to learn, and I got marvellous bit parts with very few lines. He would play the lead while I enjoyed being a foolish footman in *Le Malade Imaginaire* by Moliere, or Firs, the elderly butler in Chekhov's *The Cherry Orchard*. During these years I was gripped and mightily entertained by *The Goon Show*. I think it kept teenage depression at a distance and gave me a taste for their comically mad take on reality, a taste which has endured and matured since.

For a while I edited our house magazine, *Number 18*. It was typed up and fixed to the wall inside the entrance at No. 18 Little Dean's Yard, Wren House. This was the first of my encounters with almost serious writing and editing. The question of my awful handwriting came up again at Westminster and at one point, teachers refused to mark my work until, they said, they could read it. Unabashed I asked my mother if I could use her 1926 Royal portable typewriter. She had moved on to a lighter, more portable Olivetti Lettera 32, I think. I started to type my work and the teachers resumed marking it. Despite the repeated doom-laden warnings about my writing throughout my education, I only ever failed two examinations – O level German, which was due to simply not knowing as much as I might have done, and radar, which was probably due to my inadequate grasp of principles derived largely from magic and speculation, the foundation of much theory about radio and radar.

CHAPTER 2

Almost at sea

I left school not at all sure what to do next. I certainly didn't want any more formal education for the time being, thank you very much. My parents were disappointed that I hadn't set my sights on university. I was their last hope of a graduate child. 'I've had education up to here,' I said. But bless them, there was no drawn-out discussion. Looking back, I think my parents had a delightfully laissez-faire attitude to their children's hopes and aspirations. That written, I do remember my mother still trying to rearrange brother Ian's life well into her seventies. In discussing my progress, or lack of it, in the Church of England, she once told me that she had several bishops up her sleeve, words that painted a hilarious picture in my mind.

She did ask me one day what horse I fancied to win the 1956 Cambridgeshire Handicap. I replied that I knew nothing about racing. 'Just pick a name.' I looked at the list and said, 'Loppylugs.' The horse romped home at 50-to-1, and I won enough to put down a deposit on my first guitar.

In my last term at Westminster, Graham Stanford had asked me if I would like to spend three weeks on a trawler out of Grimsby with him. I said yes immediately. So, not knowing what to expect, we reported to Northern Trawlers' offices in Grimsby and were directed to the *Northern Spray*, an oil-fired trawler converted from coal, built in 1936 in Germany for Mac Fisheries, based at Fleetwood, part of the Lever Brothers group. She was bought by Northern Trawlers in 1937. At the outbreak of war, she was requisitioned by the Admiralty and became an anti-submarine trawler. After the war she was bought

The Northern Spray

back by Northern Trawlers for the huge sum of one pound.

Once the ship had taken on enough ice in bulk for the fish rooms, we sailed from Grimsby. We had been signed on as supernumeraries. We sailed north, and somewhere off Scotland the skipper told me that he couldn't make the Marconi radio-telephone work. This was a problem as he needed to talk to his office in Grimsby. Without a moment's hesitation I asked if I could have a crack at it. He shoved the thick manual at me and wished me good luck. I sat on the deck with my back to a bulkhead and started to read it through. I hoped that messing about with circuits and kits, starting with a crystal set then moving on to building amplifiers and other circuits, would help me make sense of this radio-telephone.

Whatever the problem was, I sorted it, and the skipper was able to talk to the office of Northern Trawlers back in Grimsby. As any sailor might know, the North Sea can be an uncomfortable place to be even in August. We rolled and bucketed our way north towards North Cape before turning east towards the White Sea and the coast of Russia.

Once we reached the fishing grounds, work started in earnest. I was told my job was to be below the main deck in the holds. The fish were gutted on the main deck and thrown down a chute into the fish rooms where I stood ready for them, with a large shovel and a bottle of orange squash and tons and tons of ice. On one occasion I turned to two minutes late and was obliged to travel down the chute from the main deck with the gutted fish. Not nice. I spent hours shovelling a layer of ice, a layer of fish, a layer of ice, a layer of fish. When we were fishing, like everyone on board I worked some eighteen hours out of every twenty-four. Meals were good, but a little unadventurous. If you are a ship's cook and fresh fish are coming aboard by the ton, why spend time thinking up original recipes? So we ate fish, fish, and more fish. On the stern, there was a boiler in which cod livers were boiled up to produce cod liver oil.

I think the crew numbered some twenty or so souls. We lived, breathed, and slept in a very confined space. Fishermen tend to be extremely superstitious. Whistling is not encouraged for fear of whistling up the wind. Language aboard was very ripe, and some days before we returned to Grimsby, the skipper told me he was very worried about what might happen when I came down to breakfast on my first day at home. He was terrified I might say to my mother, 'F***ing Hell, mother, where's the f***ing breakfast?' I assured him there was no chance of that happening. It didn't.

I don't think we caught as much fish as the owners would have liked, but fishing is both a chancy and a dangerous occupation. In the last few years, I have watched many television programmes about trawling and have been horrified at the dangers even with all the modern electronic equipment. During the war HMS *Northern Spray* had been a convoy escort regularly crossing the Atlantic. On one convoy she had picked up well over a hundred seafarers from four torpedoed merchantmen, and she was ordered to Newfoundland as she was dangerously overloaded and needed to discharge them ashore. Catching up on what happened to *Northern Spray* after I left, I learnt that it had run aground near Isafjördur on the north coast of Iceland on 23 October 1963. The crew was saved by the British trawler *James Barrie* and the Icelandic Coast Guard patrol vessel *Óðinn*. The *Northern Spray* was written off as a total loss.

When we signed off at Northern Trawlers, one of the staff, the man in charge of radio, told me that if I trained as a radio operator, Northern Trawlers would be happy to employ me. That summer, I discovered there was a college in Penywern Road, Earl's Court, The London Telegraph Training College, which offered courses for marine and airborne radio operators.

The course lasted for nine months. One of my fellow students was Richard Payne and we used to walk down to Earl's Court Road where we ate an amazing lunch for about one shilling and sixpence upstairs in Hardinge's Dining Rooms just round the corner from the Underground station. We worked together at learning all about radio operating. We studied the *Post Office Handbook for Radio Operators*, memorised call signs of the post office coast radio stations, learned about traffic lists, urgency and distress signals. We studied radio theory with an Irish lecturer who, I believe, also sold carpets to supplement his income. His manner of teaching was to dictate whole sections of the *Admiralty Handbook of Wireless Telegraphy* 1938 for us to copy into our notebooks. A more modern textbook was *Foundations of Wireless* by James Scroggie. I still have a copy of a small green book, *Worked Radio Calculations*, which looks as if I never opened it.

We learned Morse code, to send it and to receive it. The examination standard for the Postmaster General's Second-Class Certificate of Competence in Radiotelegraphy was twenty words a minute. A short dapper man, Mr King, taught Morse. We thought he completed the *Times* or the *Telegraph* crossword on his way in to work at the college.

We also had to learn fault-finding. This was taught by a Mr Savage, who wore large shoes with crepe soles, which some unkind students called Cunarders or brothel-creepers. He had very bushy eyebrows and he knew what he was talking about. He insisted that if we did any soldering, the joint should be so good you could hold up the piece of equipment by the newly soldered joint. He would disable the transmitter or receiver in the room at the bottom of the garden and then dare us to find what was wrong and put it right. He was particularly keen to see some evidence of logical thinking demonstrated by his students. We did our best.

One day I was called to the bursar's office on the top floor of this Victorian terrace house. 'Forbes,' he said, 'you must improve your handwriting, or you will not pass your examination!' I don't think I appeared sufficiently chastened as he repeated his ominous warning about the end of my career as a Sparks before it had even begun.

Came the days of the examination and we slogged our way through the technical written papers and the Morse tests and the fault-finding practical examinations. Richard Payne and I both passed and reported to Siemens Brothers of Woolwich who, in their welcome, were keen for us to know that the marine radio companies had asked the Postmaster General to lower the pass marks to let more Sparks through the examinations to lessen the shortage of radio operators. Having worked that hard to get our licence, we thought this a bit harsh and less than welcoming. Subject to passing eye tests we were taken on, told our pay would be some £32 a month. Accommodation and meals were, of course, included all the time we were signed on articles. Income tax was just one shilling in the pound, due, I imagine to the fact that we would be out of the UK's jurisdiction for several months of the year. I found I could live like a lord, pay my tax, and still save half my pay per month. This proved quite useful to my mother who borrowed some £200 to help pay for an operation at St Luke's Hospital, Chelsea.

CHAPTER 3

A life of luxury on a pound a day

I didn't go back to Northern Trawlers as I hoped that deep sea trades might be less uncomfortable. Having in the last few years seen documentary series about life aboard trawlers and all the attendant perils, I am glad I decided to go deep sea and not return to fishing. My mother took me to the naval outfitters Gieves in Bond Street to buy me a uniform and some tropical shorts and shirts.

I was put on a two-operator ship, the Royal Mail Ship *Loch Garth*, 8,617 tons, for six months. All newcomers to the trade had to spend six months with a senior radio officer before being risked on a single-operator ship. This was a dream ship to be joining. Royal Mail Lines operated a joint service with Holland America Line to the west coast of America and Canada. We carried general cargo and just twelve passengers. The days of mass cruising were still far in the future. Why twelve passengers? I discovered that a ship's doctor had to be carried if more than twelve passengers were aboard. I don't think it mattered how many seafarers were on board. One of the deck officers was trained to deal with minor medical problems, as I was to discover.

The itinerary for the voyage lasting some three months was London, Hamburg, Rotterdam, Antwerp, Bermuda, Jamaica, Panama Canal, San Diego, Los Angeles, San Francisco, Seattle, Vancouver, Victoria, New Westminster, and back to London via Glasgow and Liverpool.

The food was good because we had passengers. Breakfast would be a sequence of fresh fruit, choice of cereal, fish, bacon, eggs, sausages, tomatoes, toast, tea, or coffee. When the weather was hot, a canvas swimming pool was rigged on the foredeck, a great way of cooling off after a long night's radio watch. How I never put weight on with all that food I will never know.

The passengers depended for their grasp of news on a half-hour broadcast to shipping in the middle of the night, sent and received in Morse code from some station in England. This had to be taken down in longhand and then transcribed into typewritten text to be pinned up in one of the passenger areas by breakfast time. The challenge of Morse code is to resist the temptation to think about what you are hearing. This is especially true of receiving a news broadcast taking up to thirty minutes. The moment you wonder about one word or part of a story, you are lost. For Morse is a linear process. Miss one word, worry about it, and it has gone. In the middle of the night with the ship quiet and eyelids wanting to close, this was a significant test of my ability to concentrate. Now all those years later I can still read Morse. It is lodged somewhere deep in my brain and it is good to find I can still read at up to twenty-five words a minute. Shame that it has all but fallen out of use, except by amateur radio operators and makers of navigational aids. Morse can be read through the most atrocious noise, static, and interference. Voice transmissions are far more vulnerable.

My senior radio officer was Frank Page who had been at sea for years. His memories of sailing on Arctic convoys were fresh and scary. Because of the cold and the dangers of being torpedoed, he told me he spent much of his time lying in his bunk fully clothed with duffle coat, seaboots, and lifejacket, with headphones clamped to his ears. His hobbies at sea were building electric locomotives and listening to classical music, most of which I heard in the radio room next to his cabin.

In Vancouver we stayed some ten days while the boilers were cleaned. The city was celebrating British Columbia's centenary in 1958. Princess Margaret was due to visit the province. There was a beard-growing competition and citizens were seen with beards almost touching the pavement. In Vancouver I discovered the Missions to Seamen. The chaplain at Vancouver, Stanley Smith, was hospitable

RMS Loch Gowan – sister ship to Loch Garth

and welcoming. The Missions' chaplains and volunteers visit ships, help with any problem seafarers might have, and make them welcome ashore in seafarers' centres in some two hundred ports around the world. I have thought down the years that their work is some of the best work, hidden work done by the Anglican Church. Seafarers today are largely invisible; it's good that they have the Missions to look after their interests as well as working tirelessly on their behalf with trade unions, governments, shipowners, and the United Nations' International Maritime Organization. Later I was to learn that at least 10 per cent of shipowners are crooks and could not care less either for their ships or their seafarers.

One day somewhere off the coast of California, I reported to the second mate who was in charge of medicine. My ankles had swollen up. This had happened once before when I had a holiday job in Whitstable at the Bear and Key Hotel. I had been taken to the hospital and the duty doctor had told the ward sister that there was a lot of this about, no-one knew what it was but twelve aspirin a day and a shot of penicillin night and morning should sort it.

The second mate asked me what I thought it was, so I replied that there was a lot of it about, no-one knew what it was but twelve aspirin a day and a shot of penicillin night and morning should fix it. He measured out the aspirin and told me to bend over for the injection. I was sent ashore in the next port where a private doctor asked me what I thought it was. I responded as before, and he told me to carry on with the medication and go and see a doctor in the next port if it didn't improve. It did, so I didn't.

My time on the *Loch Garth* came to an end all too soon. She was a comfortable ship, the food was good, the itinerary interesting. My next ship was a smaller one, the Motor Vessel *Sugar Importer*, owned by Silvertown Services Shipping, some 4,000 tons, built by Hall Russell in Aberdeen. I don't know who designed the vessel but whoever it was clearly didn't know about the way ships roll. In my cabin the bed, which was otherwise comfortable, was aligned across the ship. So when the ship rolled, I was banged into the headboard or propelled towards the bed end. And that ship really rolled. I imagined becoming shorter and shorter as the voyage progressed. The accommodation was all at the stern, leaving the holds forward to be filled with thousands of tons of bulk sugar. This being a single-operator ship, I worked eight hours on watch a day. If ships sent out a distress signal when I was off watch, they would be heard by the auto-alarm receiver which would trigger an alarm to get me on watch and ready to assist in any way I could.

The voyages were six to seven weeks in duration, from London to Jamaica or Trinidad and back to Tate and Lyle's refinery at Silvertown, in the East End of London. In Jamaica we loaded sugar at either Salt River or Savanna La Mar; in Trinidad we loaded at Monkey Point.

I once was asked to describe life on board the *Sugar Importer*. I said that I thought it was a sort of licensed sea-going monastery. Beer

MV Sugar Importer

was the most expensive drink on the ship at a shilling a can. Rum, Tate and Lyle's own Caroni brand, was seven shillings a bottle. Each of us officers was given a free bottle of rum per voyage. Cigarettes sold for twelve shillings for ten packets of twenty. Luckily for me I had never taken to smoking, despite being offered the chance to smoke a cigarette in the toilet of a school train taking us to Eastbourne in 1947. Where we loaded sugar, we anchored rather than being tied up at a wharf, which meant that loading could take several days. Sugar was brought down to the wharf where it was transferred to barges which were then towed out to the ship, and loaded using the ship's derricks.

Both the *Loch Garth* and the *Sugar Importer* sailed through the most appalling weather and crockery breakages and danger to elderly lives and limbs were the subject of many anxious conversations. Technically care of both crew and passengers was the responsibility of the shipping line. I remember after one very stormy crossing of the Atlantic in *Loch Garth*, we landed the passengers in Liverpool, at Huskisson Dock, and as one passenger was assisted down the gangway, I heard a collective sigh of relief from the officers as he stood briefly on the dock. He had suffered from a bad fall during a storm and there were anxieties about his health as a result.

The captain I sailed with most often in the *Sugar Importer* was a marvellous man, Captain Eddie Moses. He had been through World War Two, and there was little if anything he didn't know about the sea and ships. He told me how to make a bottle of gin go very much further. He had been taught how to do this in North Africa before the end of the war: Take a bottle of Gordon's London Gin and empty it out to the level of the embossed lettering on the back of the bottle. Carefully pare the rind of an orange or lemon, feed the rind into the neck of the bottle, and push it down into the gin. Pour a cupful of white sugar into the bottle and top it up with the gin removed earlier. If there is gin left over, enjoy it. Put the top on the bottle, shake it once or twice a day for six weeks, and your orange or lemon liqueur will be ready.

Once in a hurricane off the coast of Cuba, I was standing on the bridge and Captain Moses said to me, 'Patrick, I don't think she's coming back from this one.' There was a clinometer on the bulkhead which measured the roll of the ship from the vertical, and this had registered a roll of some sixty or more degrees. Had we been loaded with a full cargo of sugar, I think we would have sunk. Being in ballast, the ship rolled back from that terrible angle. The hurricane was a scary thing and as it moved, the eye of the storm passed over the ship. As if a switch had been pulled, the sea almost flattened and for a matter of minutes, there was little obvious evidence of the storm. Then as the eye moved away from us, it all started up again, howling winds, mountainous seas. Looking back, I don't find it at all surprising that so many seafarers are spiritual in one way or another. They see the forces of nature at their best and at their worst and have days and weeks in which to reflect on the experience.

When the sugar season ended in the Caribbean, we would sail

down to South Africa for sugar. One year the *Sugar Importer* was in dry dock in Antwerp. We were expecting to sail just before Christmas to Rouen before sailing south. A new deck crew came out to Antwerp from London to sign on. Almost to a man, once they saw the ship, hull fully exposed in dry dock, and maybe thinking they would rather be at home for Christmas, they turned and caught the ferry back to London.

So, we signed on seafarers – French, German, a Dane, a Spaniard from Seville who, it turned out, was working at sea to save up enough money to become a barber in his hometown. We left Antwerp and were bucketing down the English Channel on Christmas Day in a foul storm. I was sitting in the radio room on watch when Captain Moses came in and asked if I had a couple of frightening looking tools. I asked why, and he told me that the seafarers were marking Christmas with a knife and broken-bottle fight below. He needed to go and restore some semblance of order. I found him an enormous Swedish steel shifting spanner and a half-rubber strop insulator which had a nylon core and an eye moulded for a shackle at one end, a vicious weapon. He went below and returned some half-hour later to say that all was peace and quiet below.

Meanwhile in the galley on the ship's stern, the cook was performing heroically, preparing a Christmas dinner for the crew of thirty-two. Imagine working on an open range with large pots of potatoes and Brussels sprouts as your kitchen rises and falls tens of feet and rolls from side to side. It was a delicious meal, and the cook should have received a medal for his efforts.

CHAPTER 4

Falling in love – and much more

After a year or more at sea, Richard Payne, with whom I had studied for a second-class certificate at Earl's Court, and I agreed to come ashore and study for a first-class certificate. Siemens were happy, though we would not be paid while studying but we would be kept on their books. We discovered that we could draw unemployment benefit. We enrolled at Norwood Technical College. I stayed with three other students in a flat above a wool shop on Bellevue Parade, facing Wandsworth Common. The shop was owned by the mother of a friend I had made at Westminster School, Andrew Cheyne. He and his two friends were studying at Imperial College. Each of us had an old car, mine being quite the most disreputable, a 1933 Austin 7 that I had bought for £15. We had an agreement that if the day ever came when our four cars could drive around Wandsworth Common at the same time, we would celebrate with something more than our habitual lunch of a cheese roll and a Mackeson stout in the Surrey Tavern, our local just a few doors along from the wool shop. It happened only once!

Richard Payne and I made friends with some of our fellow students at Norwood Technical College and among them was Peter Beech who was studying electronics. He was in love with Avril Snape, daughter of a professional singer. Peter and Avril were keen to attend the Student Union's summer dance at Lambeth Town Hall in Brixton. Avril would be staying with a friend, Annette Miller, who lived with her parents in Upper Norwood. I was asked if I would like to make up a foursome. Without a moment's hesitation, I said yes.

Annette had trained at Catherine Judson's Secretarial College at around the time I had been training in Earl's Court. When we met, she was working in the Religious Broadcasting Department of the BBC. She worked for the Reverend Elsie Chamberlain, a Congregational minister married to an Anglican priest, Norman Garrington. Elsie was a producer responsible for *Lift Up Your Hearts*, *The Silver Lining* with Stuart Hibberd, and the *Daily Service*. The BBC had outgrown Broadcasting House and the department occupied part of the first floor of the former hotel, The Langham, on the opposite side of the road.

Annette and her mother were members of All Saints Church, Upper Norwood. We went there together, and churchgoing suddenly became very attractive indeed.

In October 1959 I gained my first-class certificate of competence in radiotelegraphy and I must have gone back to sea soon after my twenty-first birthday in November. By then, Annette and I were an item, and the idea was that I would go back to sea to save up for when we would marry.

I joined the *Sugar Refiner*, at 5,104 tons and launched in 1958 a slightly bigger bulk sugar carrier. This too had been built by Hall Russell of Aberdeen. I had a very pleasant cabin, with a bunk installed fore and aft with drawers beneath. The bulkheads were Formica, handy when removing the corpses of mosquitoes.

I settled back into life at sea, but now writing letters to Annette and anxiously awaiting replies. When I knew when we would be docking at Plaistow Wharf Refinery, I would call her office at the BBC to find out if she could get time off for the thirty-six hours or so I might be in London. If her manager, Doris English, was merciful, Annette would have some time off and we would meet and distribute the duty-free allowance of cigarettes, rum, whisky, or gin to our families, and catch up with each other.

It was clear that I would not be spending many more years at sea. Annette wasn't prepared to be a seafarer's wife. I could understand that. Very few wives ever got to sail with their husbands then. And what was there for their husbands to do in their off-duty hours? At sea, there were cigarettes and alcohol and hours with nothing much more to do than dream of home or of the reported delights of a few hours off in some foreign port far from home. While I was at sea, I had seen or heard of many marriages breaking down. Looking back, I am not that surprised. At sea now, there are far better facilities for keeping in touch with homes and families – ships being equipped with satellite systems – though access to these will depend on the management's policy towards their seafarers and their ability to pay. Crews being smaller, ships being faster, there are added pressures on seafarers, facts I would learn much later in life. I was lucky to have been at sea when ships were slower, crews were larger, and there was time to read maybe two books a day and think and relax in between hurricanes, foul weather, and runs and leaves ashore.

One of the nightmares of being a ship's radio officer was the possibility of having a medical emergency while at sea. I mentioned earlier the responsibility that one officer might have, presumably having been on a course to enable him to know what to do with accidents and emergencies of a medical nature. I could imagine the worst-case scenario of a seafarer needing to have his appendix removed at sea, or worse, an amputation. I tried to imagine my role in such a situation, having to get instructions in Morse code from some distant, shore-based medical facility. Two examples of near-emergency stick in my mind. One was the captain coming to the radio room at night when the ship was leaping all over the place in a nasty North Atlantic winter storm. 'Sparks, get on the radio to Portishead,' he said, closing the door behind him and looking around the matchbox-sized radio room to make sure no-one else would hear what he said. Portishead was the UK's major long-distance high-frequency radio station for ships at sea. 'The chief engineer looks as if he has got typhoid. We need to find out whether he really has got it, and what drug in the ship's medical chest should be given to him. Quick as you can.'

I turned on the ship's main transmitter and called Portishead. No reply. I kept trying and eventually heard from Malta Naval Radio. They said that they had passed my message on to Portishead, it looked like typhoid to them, but I should wait to hear direct from Portishead.

Eventually I was just able to hear Portishead. They spelt out the name of the drug to be administered. I swear it was over twenty-six letters long. I remember thinking, 'one letter misplaced, we'll give him the wrong drug and probably kill him.' Anyway, it turned out that it wasn't typhoid but something with very similar symptoms. We gave him the drug as prescribed and he recovered, though I fancy he didn't sail with us again. The thought of treating and containing an outbreak of typhoid on a small ship thousands of miles from home was just another nightmare to add to the list.

On another voyage down to South Africa, we had left a West African port, perhaps Dakar or Abidjan, when the first mate asked me to get on the radio to the port authorities to ask for advice and assistance. One of the crew had not turned to for work and was discovered in his bunk clutching his stomach in considerable agony. I switched on the medium-frequency transmitter and started to call the coast radio station. Then the transmitter failed. I quickly established that the fault was in the keying circuit. There was no time to find the offending part and solder in a new component. I unlocked and drew out the tray with all the high-voltage parts of the output stage of the transmitter. I asked the captain to spread a towel over the tray to prevent my being electrocuted, and keyed the transmitter manually using the flap of the relay that should have been operated by the Morse key. This relay applied the voltage to the output valves of the transmitter. Improvisation can often solve problems and work miracles.

We were answered by the coast radio station who told us to return to the port at the best speed we could manage. They would have an ambulance ready to rush the sailor to hospital for surgery. This we did, and the last we heard was that he was recovering from his operation and being flown home to Holland.

From time to time, we ferried guests of the company to or from the West Indies. One such was a missionary for the United Society for the Propagation of the Gospel, the Reverend Robert Nind, who had been appointed to a parish in Jamaica. One Sunday on the voyage to Jamaica, he celebrated communion in the day room on the ship. I was there and I think there was one other member of the crew. Although the day was fine and sunny, the swell and the ship's rolling meant I had to try to prevent the Communion wine being spilt.

On subsequent voyages, I asked the chief steward if we could put together boxes of English food, corn flakes, marmalade, and other goods that might be beyond Bob's budget on his missionary stipend. He agreed and this missionary aid was delivered to Bob at his home. Months later in one of his letters to me on board, he said that he hoped that he would one day see my name on a list of those to be ordained priest in the Church of England. I was both shocked and a little puzzled as ordination could not have been further from my mind at the time. Life at sea was far too interesting. Yes, I was interested in faith, having joined Annette's church, All Saints, Upper Norwood but in my wildest nightmares I had never thought of being a priest.

My time at sea left me with a sense of love and wonder at creation. Born by the sea in Somerset, the sea was slowly making its mark on me. Every morning, it might be the same sea, but we would have moved on and it always looked different, mysterious, and powerful. Sunrise and sunset and the weather in all its moods gripped me like nothing else. I saw the sea and my fellow men at their very best and sometimes at their very worst, and I could not help but wonder at the courage and determination to get safely from one place to another no matter what the elements or circumstances threw our way.

CHAPTER 5

Ashore, marriage, and then . . .

I came ashore for good in 1961 and eventually found work with a company breaking into the telephone answering machine business, Robophone Ltd. I was sent to the company's factory in Battersea from the Labour Exchange. The job was a bench fitter and the pay eight pounds a week. I was interviewed by the factory manager, a Mr Matthews. I was quite puzzled by his questions. 'Do you have a driver's licence, do you like meeting people, do you like travelling?' Why these questions for a bench fitting job, I wondered.

I walked away from that interview as a service and installation engineer, with a company vehicle and fifteen pounds a week. Three weeks later the factory manager was sacked. Could it have been because he had employed me? I soon discovered that there was only one other such engineer, Dave Rands. Between us we were responsible for installation and servicing these machines throughout the UK. In the fourteen months I worked for Robophone, I clocked up some 34,000 miles and that was just the driving, the easy bit, not the meetings with enraged customers who felt let down by the machine they rented from us.

Only some way into my employment did I discover that, as I was driving one of the firm's vehicles, I was supposed to keep an official log of miles driven, rest breaks taken. No one had bothered to tell me about this legal requirement or if they did, I must have been asleep at the time. I acquired a logbook and put everything down in it exactly as it happened. I wasn't going to add the telling of lies to the crime of driving too far for too long!

I was once asked by the company to drive to Birmingham in the snow to deliver some machines to the office there. I protested that it wouldn't be safe as the handbrake on my van didn't work and was due to be repaired. The thought of driving in the snow without a serviceable handbrake did not appeal. They said, 'Either you go, or we'll sack you.' So, shocked and grumbling, I went. As I was recently married, I could not afford to lose my job.

Matters came to a head after I had spent a week servicing and installing machines in Scotland. I was driving out of Glasgow on the Dunbarton Road at, I think, fifty-two miles per hour and I was stopped by a policeman who said I would be charged with speeding. I drove across to Edinburgh and south down the A1 to London. I knew if I took all Saturday to drive down, I wouldn't get that day back from the company. I think I arrived home in Crystal Palace at about half past four on the Saturday morning, having driven through the night.

I was eventually summoned to appear in Glasgow Sheriff's court to answer the charge of speeding. If I was not to appear, I had to send my driving licence together with a letter with any plea in mitigation. I had written to the company, explaining what had happened and asking that they review the hours we spent driving, which were in excess of those allowed by law. Interestingly and perhaps predictably they did not bother to reply. I kept a copy of the letter I had sent to them.

I sent my licence to Glasgow with a letter explaining how hard the company worked us and how they had not replied to my letter to them, a copy of which I enclosed. I eventually received my driving licence back unmarked with a letter saying that I had not been fined but that I had been admonished by the court.

Years later, in 1966, because I was a prison visitor in Lincoln, I had joined the Howard League for Penal Reform. The Howard League organised a Congress on Crime to take place in London. As a member I was eligible to attend and I went. I kept a running record of both the press coverage together with notes I made during the conference. One of the seminars was concerned with motoring and crime. In the discussion after the lecture, I asked a question concerning the plight of drivers who were worked criminally hard by their employers, making clear without mentioning names that the question was based on my own experience some years earlier.

During the coffee break, I was approached by a police superintendent from Scotland. He introduced himself to me and said, 'Don't tell me the name of the firm you worked for. It was Robophone, wasn't it?' I confessed that it was and wondered how he knew this. He explained that after the court case at the Glasgow Sheriff's Court, the court had written to all the police forces in Scotland, summarising the findings of the court and asking that Robophone vans and drivers be watched for and challenged if thought to be in breach of the law. Feedback can work, which was refreshing to learn.

Annette and I were married at All Saints Church, Upper Norwood by the vicar, the Reverend Michael Percival Smith. We had found a

The wedding party: left to right, my parents, Bill and Evie Forbes, the happy couple, and Annette's parents, May and Bob Miller.

flat at five pounds a week underneath the ballroom of the Queen's Hotel, Crystal Palace. It was called Garden Flat 2. Annette's father had booked the wedding reception to happen in the Queen's Hotel itself. Three weeks before the wedding on 16 June 1962, Robert Miller went to check that all was well with the booking. It wasn't. The hotel told him there had been a booking error on their part and that the reception couldn't happen there. They had not thought to let him know.

Somehow, he managed to book a reception at three weeks' notice at the Selsdon Park Hotel, a very posh place in splendid grounds, perhaps better known as the venue for a meeting of the Conservative Party shadow cabinet in early 1970 than as our wedding reception venue of second choice. It was six and a half miles from All Saints Church, and my best man Richard Payne and I took our 1936 Austin 7 Nippy down there the night before the wedding. Next morning, because Annette and I were crossing the Channel to honeymoon in Normandy, we thought it best to look for a pair of spare half-shafts for the car before we left. Richard and I toured car parts shops and breakers' yards in South London before arriving at my parents' house in Westbridge Road, Battersea, in time for a hurried lunch before setting out for the church. We were extremely lucky to find a pair of brand-new half-shafts in their oiled wrapper for a car built some twenty-six years earlier. I just knew that if we didn't take them with us to France, if one broke we wouldn't be able to acquire another one there.

Since coming ashore, I had become more and more involved in All Saints Church. I even got to attend an annual church meeting. When it came to any other business, to my surprise I found myself on my feet bitterly complaining about the state of the toilets in the church hall. I remember saying that if the church hall was a trawler, it wouldn't be allowed to sail with its wooden lavatory seats! Annette and I helped with the youth club and baby-sat for the curate Stephen MacDonald and his wife Jill. I remember speaking to the Church of England Men's Society about ethics at work, citing my experience with Robophone. At a church fete I had my first outing as half a pantomime horse, just for fun.

People started to say, 'You ought to think about ordination, Patrick.' First a missionary on a ship in the Atlantic, then members of a South London church congregation, what was God thinking of? The suggestion came as a shock. I'm sure the vicar, Michael Smith, was a great influence on my agreeing to look into the possibility of ordination. I don't remember being interviewed by any diocesan officer about this change of direction. I have a hazy memory of meeting our local bishop, Bishop John Taylor Hughes of Croydon, an amiable chap who saw me at his club near Trafalgar Square.

To try and sort this out I applied to the Central Advisory Council for Training for the Ministry, filled in the odd form, and waited to see what might happen. I had to list qualifications, details of present and previous employment. I received a letter to say that the church authorities had not been able to assess my technical qualifications in academic terms. It was not a question I had imagined mattering that much. I don't think I was ever seen by a Director of Ordinands or any other diocesan official. Perhaps that was just as well; I might not have leapt over any such obstacles placed in my troubled, hesitant path.

While all this was going on, I was beginning to look for a more enjoyable, less stressful job. An advertisement appeared for a technical engineer to work for IBC Sound Recording Studios, in Langham Place, just up from the BBC where Annette was working.

I was interviewed for this position and admitted that there was just a chance I might be selected for ordination training. This did not appear to be a problem for them. Maybe they thought that pigs might well fly before I was chosen.

The new job was great. The studio, one of the best equipped in Europe, handled all kinds of work, station identifications for United States commercial radio stations, Shakespeare plays, classical and pop music. I was a member of the workshop team headed by Dennis King, assisted by Peter Smith. Every day there was something different to do. When we were not working in the studio or the control room, we would be building circuits designed by Dennis either for IBC or one of their customers. We once had an order for some limiters to be built for Philips Records. We designed and built the coil winders we needed for this project.

One of the more bizarre projects was the dreaded Mellotron, a mechanical electronic synthesizer. Built like any upright piano, its innards were a complex blend of tape transport mechanisms and electronic circuitry. The keys looked like those of any piano, but instruments could be selected as could any number of rhythms and accompaniments. Our role was mercifully limited to recording the master tapes. I was on duty one evening when some piano tracks were to be recorded. The studio's chairman was Eric Robinson, a television personality who presented television programmes such as *Music for You*. He and the managing director and musician George Clouston could not agree on whether the grand piano in the studio was in tune. After some time, it was decided late in the evening that it wasn't, and it was agreed we should adjourn to Eric's house in Hampstead where recordings could be made using his piano. We drove there with microphones, a portable mixer, and cables and a tape machine. I think I finally got home at three the next morning. Waking later than usual, but with good reason, I thought, I reported for work at around 11 a.m., only to be summoned to the manager's office. He asked why I had not come in to work on time. I explained about the Mellotron session nightmare of the night before and the fact that I had only got home to bed six hours before being expected to be back at nine o'clock. I was told firmly that I should have reported at 9 a.m. as usual and then be sent home to catch up on sleep. Oh dear.

The Mellotron was eventually released to the public and saw some service before being rendered redundant by fully electronic synthesisers such as those made by Moog, Yamaha, and Korg. I believe that one was used to good effect by the BBC as an easier source of sound effects for their work on *The Goon Show*. When sold, the first models cost around £1,000, at a time when houses could be bought for between £2,000 and £3,000. I was glad that we were not involved with the design or manufacture of the machines. Our role was limited to recording the master tapes.

When the musical *Oh! What a Lovely War* opened in London, Dennis King had been set the task of designing a completely accident- and fool-proof system for playing the sound effects into the production. For this we butchered three Ferrograph recorders, each with its own identical sound effects tape, with the effects separated by sections of metal tape spliced together. If one tape machine ran more slowly than the other two, the foils would hold the two faster machine tapes so the slower one caught up. There were three identical power amplifiers fed by the tape machines. What could possibly go wrong? I was on standby in the workshop one evening when a call came from the theatre. 'It won't work,' the stage manager reported, 'come at once.'

One thing I learned from Dennis was never to panic. If the control room upstairs rang down with a problem, Dennis would say he would sort something out, and always walked, never ran, upstairs. This has proved to be a very valuable lesson.

On this occasion I took a taxi down to Wyndham's Theatre to find backstage in danger of meltdown. Actors were milling about, the front of house manager was shouting, 'it's filling up, when will it be fixed?' I settled down and asked them to move away and keep quiet so I could sort it out. Which I did, and order was restored, and the show started on time. You would think they might have offered me a free seat to see the show I had rescued! They did not.

While I was enjoying this new job, some progress was being made with the possible path to ordination. Eventually someone decided that I should attend a selection conference to see whether the whole idea was inspired or plain daft. This weekend conference took place in Cheltenham at a retreat house. Maybe just getting there in my Austin 7 would be taken as a significant achievement in any assessment they might make of me.

Each of the potential ordinands faced several interviews, the scariest of which was that with the lay selector. This selector was, I suspect, an ex-military man with more than a hint of the parade ground or court martial about him. He saw us in alphabetical order. His first victims left his room in a combination of panic and despair, white-faced and shaking. We were not supposed to talk about either the selectors or the interviews. But this seemed the time for the setting aside of the rules.

This man did not mince his words. The hapless interviewee had barely entered the room, it was said, before the lay selector barked at him, 'You're the curate, not been long in the parish. One day the doorbell rings. There's your organist on the doorstep. Says he's been raped by the choir-mistress. What are YOU going to do about it?' I fantasised about what questions I might face when he got to surnames beginning with F.

I needn't have worried. He was struck down among the Ds and Es and was not seen again. Instead, my interview was a gentle conversation with a selection secretary from Church House in London, called Murray Irvine. I can't remember what we talked about, time at sea, early experience of church. I was probably so relieved at not having to sort out the lay selector's imagined parish problems, that I may have developed such an impressive theory of divine intervention that I gave all the right answers.

One of the last exercises struck me as almost as bizarre. All the selectors and potential ordinands sat around in a large comfortable drawing room. We were asked to discuss the knotty question or dilemma posed by being asked after a Sunday service of matins to join a member of the congregation at his home for a glass of sherry. As I have never taken to matins, I couldn't imagine a greater act of kindness. I could not see any ethical problem with the invitation. Others thought that one should retire to the vicarage for perhaps twenty minutes before turning up to partake of sherry. I am sure that I couldn't see the point of that and probably said so.

Some people look back on their lives and see individual dates or occurrences which made all the difference to their faith journey. I can do no such thing. When asked, I retreat to describing my path as being like rising damp, osmosis, a gradual, sometimes hesitant, almost backwards progress towards the wild idea of being a priest in the Church of England. Certainly there were days when I thought the work at the recording studio was so enjoyable, and at times demanding, that ordination might never happen.

There were perhaps two to four weeks of near anxiety to hear whether the selectors had recommended me for ordination training or not. Eventually a letter arrived to say that they had and that I should start looking for a theological college to train me. I am told that the pass rate from such selection conferences stands at around 50 per cent, with many a story of a lack of pastoral care for those whose hopes of ordination had been dashed by a formal letter after the conference. I imagine and hope there may have been any number of discussions about the selection processes employed by the Church of England. Perhaps they should look again at how someone such as I could have been let through. Presumably God has broad shoulders and can cope with the consequences of such decisions. I hope and trust so.

My parish priest, who had married us at All Saints Church, Upper Norwood, Michael Smith, suggested I try for Cuddesdon College, just outside Oxford. I wrote to them and they invited us to see them.

On a showery Saturday we drove our 1929 Austin Chummy out to Cuddesdon from South London. We were made welcome and shown around the College. Over a pleasant cup of tea in front of a roaring fire, Robert Runcie, the principal, said, 'You probably know that only in very rare cases do we accept nongraduates here. I suggest you try Chichester.' We got into our little car and drove home.

I think I looked at Bishop's College, Cheshunt, which, I learn, closed in 1968. Michael Smith suggested the college where he had trained as had his curate Stephen MacDonald, Westcott House in Cambridge. Annette and I arranged to visit the college while staying the weekend with friends in Cambridge. The college knew that Annette had come to Cambridge with me. She was not invited in to see the college, much less to meet any of the staff. The principal, Peter Walker, spoke to me before I left and said, 'You do know that, supposing we were to offer you a place, you would have to live apart from your wife for the first year here.' I didn't wait to see if he would offer me a place and told him exactly what I thought about such an idea. Peter Walker went on to be a bishop.

I began to think we might be running out of colleges. We wrote to Alan Webster, warden of the Bishop's Hostel, Lincoln. He warmly invited us up to Lincoln one weekend. We would stay in his house and eat with the family and we could see what the college was like. On the Sunday afternoon he thanked us both for coming and told us to go home and think about whether we wanted to come to Lincoln, and to let him know if we did. He would immediately start looking for somewhere we both could live.

As soon as we got home, we wrote to say we would love to go to Lincoln which not only recognised the married state but made provision for it. Nothing had been said about my being a nongraduate and it didn't seem to be a problem, until, that is, we were about to leave college some two years later.

We were due to move to Lincoln in time for the new academic year in autumn 1964. Annette didn't move at the beginning of term as 3 Minster Yard wasn't ready for us both. She stayed with her parents in Lower Willingdon just outside Eastbourne, and she worked as a secretary at the Cavendish Hotel.

CHAPTER 6

Back to school

Annette moved up to Lincoln when our flat in 3 Minster Yard was ready for us. She quickly found a job as secretary to an architectural practice with an office between our flat and the college. College was very strange, going back to school in a sort of almost grown-up way. There were all kinds of customs and traditions which took a while to get used to. The college had once been a hospital. It was called the Bishop's Hostel. Those who were thought likely to die were accommodated on the top floor, I was told, when later I moved to a room up a winding stair in a turret above the terminal second floor. Nearer, my God, to thee.

The student body was split roughly half and half between married men and bachelors. I don't know if the bachelors resented the efforts made by the college to integrate the wives into the community. I suspect there was some friction. I remember blustery days when every time I turned a corner of the Minster, the wind force increased by a factor of one on the Beaufort Scale. I guess there was little between the Ural Mountains of Russia and the hill on which Lincoln Minster was built.

During my first year I said less and listened more in wonder at the curious language of theology graduates, some of whom probably couldn't see why they had to endure more endless lectures on doctrine, church history, Old Testament, New Testament, New Testament Greek, Christian worship, and ethics before being let loose on a parish.

Theological language was peppered with all manner of technical terms such as *anaphora, anamnesis, teleological,* and *hermeneutic.* Years later when I studied sociology, I realized that most professions have

Lincoln Theological College

their own secret language or jargon which no-one else understands, nor should they be allowed to lest they understand and see through the whole nonsense. I concluded that jargon if it had to be used should be limited to consenting adults, preferably in private.

One student, Brian, with whom I shared a room, developed a great facility for revision. During lectures he would doze off. His pen stayed on the page; when he woke up, the pen started moving again. When he came to revise, he had fewer notes to read through, with perhaps the most boring bits excised as he had slept through them. I wish I had had that kind of skill. My notes were much longer so I had to spend more time reading them than he did with his sleep edited notes.

The fact that I had studied and passed O level Classical Greek was undoubtedly a blessing, something I hadn't quite understood when my father had told me if I wanted to be a journalist, I should study Latin and Greek. While working at IBC Studios, I arrived early enough to spend an hour with New Testament Greek before starting the day's work. When I had had enough of *New Testament Greek: An Introductory Grammar* by Eric G. Jay, I would read *The Guardian*. The Vietnam War and many other stories reinforced my growing conviction that there had to be a better way of running the world.

Eric Jay's book helped me pass the Greek examination at Lincoln. Some students for whom Greek was a great trial were conditionally ordained, on the shaky assumption that there would be time for Greek catch-up in their first parishes. The joke is on me and the Church of England in that for all my studies, I am almost certain that a familiarity with Greek has been of very little, if any, use to me in my ministry.

Lincoln had a pleasant chapel where we said morning and evening prayer, followed by compline to end the day. On summer Saturdays, there was more than a hint of peppermint in the chapel as some of the more cricketing students tried to combat the evidence of hours spent in some pub or cricket pavilion.

The college founded by Edward Benson in 1874 had Tractarian or High Church origins. Once or twice a year, incense was used on a Sunday morning at the college Eucharist. Because it was so infrequently used, no-one could get it quite right. Either there was too much incense and the sanctuary party vanished within a dense cloud of smoke and much coughing was heard, or there was but a pathetic wisp of smoke ascending like a failed prayer. Alan Webster, the warden, thought it mattered to discover which if any of the students might be allergic to incense before they joined a parish where incense was a regular ingredient of worship. I have since discovered that while incense causes Annette to cough, it is also said to be disliked by bats.

Once a year there was a brutal football match against Kelham Theological College, near Nottingham. No holds were barred, and the match looked more like a medieval battle between Crusaders and Infidels. Many and varied were the injuries sustained before the match ended and we joined our rivals for slabs of cake and mugs of tea before an angelic sung evensong in their splendid chapel.

All students had to engage in hospital visiting in their first year. After that they could choose to be a prison visitor, help in a local borstal, or continue hospital visiting. I couldn't wait to have an alternative. I found hospital visiting challenging. I wasn't too sure that anyone particularly wanted to see me. I may have been a bit shy. I may have been a bit right.

I applied to be a prison visitor at Her Majesty's Prison, Lincoln, a grim Victorian institution. I was appointed in July 1965 and had to sign the Official Secrets Act. I am still not sure why. One of the few delights of prison visiting, though delight may be a strange word to use in connection with prisons, was the fact that I never saw a prisoner in his cell unless he had requested a visit. This was such a contrast with hospital visiting. In the great tradition of no-one in England being beyond the possibility of pastoral care by the Church of England by virtue of simply living in a parish, every patient might expect to be seen by a chaplain at some point during their stay, almost whether they wanted to or not. In those days, stickers of different shapes or colours indicated whether the patient was Roman Catholic, Jewish, Nonconformist, or C of E. The story is told of a general inspecting a squad of new recruits. He asks a soldier what church he belongs to. Quick as a flash the recruit replies 'C of E, sir.' 'Why the C of E?' The reply comes, 'It's cheaper, sir.'

People who have never been inside a prison sometimes hold the most extreme views about the point and purpose of prison. They think that life in prison is one long holiday, that televisions should be removed from prisons, mobile phones and telephone calls to families and friends should be banned, and that prisoners should be more severely punished. Maybe they don't understand that prison means losing the liberty that most of us enjoy. Loss of liberty is the punishment, separation from loved ones, family, and friends is to my mind punishment enough. Rehabilitation, I supposed, should be a means of learning not to offend. But when tabloids bay for blood and breaking rocks, and budgets are cut, it is education and rehabilitation that suffer. Yes, there are criminals who must never be freed because they are an utter danger to society, but I suspect that most people in prison gain nothing from it, and probably shouldn't be there anyway. And it seems to me more and more obvious that the people who are dangerous are out and about, laying down the law, organizing our every move. Our penal system costs several arms and legs, and needs root and branch reform. While a prison visitor, I joined the Howard League for Penal Reform, something much more needed now than ever it was then, when prisons held less than half the numbers they do today.

One of the more stretching activities at college was the sermon class where students wrote and delivered sermons and then suffered such criticism as fellow students might muster. In the worst cases these sermons were re-runs of academic essays, which might just be acceptable to a congregation of theology academics used to reading such essays but to the run-of-the-mill congregation member, they might be as inspiring as a pile of dead leaves, while not smelling so sweet.

Every student had to preach a trial sermon in one or other of the local churches in Lincoln with which the college had some sort of relationship. My turn came and I was required to preach for no longer than twelve minutes at a church, St Peter at Gowts, down in the town. Somewhere in the congregation at evensong there was a theology graduate with the highly appropriate name of Miss Judge who would report on what she had seen and heard to the college warden.

I carefully prepared the sermon and timed it while declaiming it to a mirror in my room. Twelve minutes. Unfortunately, I had neither been told or realized that acoustics, setting, and the presence of real people listening might affect the speed at which the sermon was given. Back came the report to the college. TOO LONG was engraved across the report sheet in large capital letters. That was what I remember of the feedback. I think it had lasted sixteen minutes, shock horror.

Years and years later I was asked by the Simeon Trustees to research sermons, the business of preaching, and write a paper for The College of Preachers. I learned how others put sermons together, about content, timing, delivery, feedback, all of which was informed by my training and work with radio production and contributing to radio religion slots. I am not sure just how helpful these college sermon classes were. Some of the criticisms offered were extremely negative. Maybe we deserved them. Certainly, it was possible to discover who one's friends and enemies might be.

More interesting and entertaining than the day-to-day lectures were the two parish visits that students made during the holidays. The first of these was to St Paul's Hartcliffe, a large housing estate on the edge of Bristol. I remember that we students were asked to become involved with a family service to mark the parish's harvest festival. I offered to prepare a talking vegetable marrow who would interrupt the vicar's sermon and try to help the congregation to understand what the fruit and vegetables might be making of the service. I glued some grass to the top of the marrow for hair, added a carrot for a nose and crouched in the pulpit to await my cue. I think it sort of worked as one part of a lively service.

I remember more of the second parish visit which was to Rotherham. Here we stayed with members of a church congregation. We were taken on several interesting trips. We visited a coal mine, Maltby Main, where we travelled down to the coalface, which was hot, noisy, and very busy. We were taken behind the scenes at a crematorium. The staff were keen that we understood that they were not, as some thought, devilish operators with horns, tails, and pitchforks.

We also visited a steelworks, Steel, Peech and Tozer, where we saw slabs of red-hot metal being rolled and hammered. That was much more the setting for the devils of hell than the crematorium. There was noise, heat, and, I imagine, some considerable risk.

Lincolnshire had a steelworks nearer than Rotherham, that of Appleby Frodingham at Scunthorpe. Some students went and spent some time there and after a few days, it seemed, they returned knowing exactly everything about steelmaking and how it might be improved and reformed. Most of the students had come to the college from school or university. I particularly enjoyed meeting a student who was to spend just a year at the college. He was sixty, and when asked what he had done before coming to Lincoln, he would smile and say that he had been forty years in sewerage. A great answer defying anyone to come up with another question. During my time there, there were few students who had come from another employment. One had been an officer in the Rhodesian police force. One had graduated with a degree in pharmacy, yet another had been a Royal Navy officer.

From time to time there were college lectures given by visiting celebrities. During my second year I became College President, a sort of dogsbody role, which included looking after visitors to the college. One of our guests was Maurice Wood, Bishop of Norwich. He was an evangelical bishop and in his lecture to us he told us about missions he had conducted while travelling on railway trains. He was dressed immaculately. During his lecture he produced leaflets and tracts from his jacket and waistcoat pockets which, he said, he gave to passengers he had met on these trains.

When his lecture finished, I rose to thank him on behalf of the college and to ask if he would accept questions. He said he would. There was a silence from those present, perhaps still processing the concept of missions on trains. 'While my fellow students are putting together their theological questions for you, Bishop,' I said, 'perhaps you could answer mine.' He nodded so I asked him who his tailor was, having been so impressed by the cut of his suit and the number of leaflets and tracts he had produced during his lecture. There was a gale of laughter in which he joined, the ice was broken, and the questions and answers flowed back and forth.

While at Lincoln I took several holiday jobs to help with living costs. One of these was working in a gentlemen's outfitters in the run up to Christmas. As a parting gift from the management, I was asked to choose a tie for myself. Of course, it had an elephant pattern. Another employment was working for Lindsey County Council's highways department. Much of the work was sitting on a tall stool at a sloping desk, left over, I imagine from Victorian times, plotting road accident statistics. Lincolnshire being farming country there was even a well-used report category for accidents involving farm livestock. My one achievement while there was reducing a set of forms from twelve pages down to just one. For a treat one day I was taken out to a scene of a road accident where I stood in some peril in the middle of a road while measurements were taken to help decide whether improvements might make the road safer at that point. Back in the office I found sitting on a high stool extremely uncomfortable and very constipating.

A more interesting work was four summer weeks spent as a temporary nursing assistant at St John's Hospital, Bracebridge Heath, an enormous Victorian mental hospital on the road from Lincoln to Sleaford. Opened in 1852, at its peak it could house some 1,900 patients. It was closed in 1989. I was assigned to a male ward where some thirty or more patients lived. Most of them could do absolutely nothing for themselves. This meant we had to wash them, bath them, get them dressed, help them with eating. I think all of them were thoroughly institutionalised, having been there for decades. I don't ever remember seeing anyone visiting them. The charge nurse knew each one of them. They were for all intents and purposes his children. The chief agent of control seemed to be enormous dollops of chlorpromazine, trade name Largactil, a pinkish fluid. I could imagine it being delivered to a network of Victorian mental hospitals by tanker, or maybe during half-terms when the school custard delivery underground pipelines were being rested.

One day, the charge nurse said, 'Patrick, see that group of patients over there. I want you to shave them.' I imagined any number of severed heads rolling around the floor. When I shave myself, I know if I have cut myself. I set these visions on one side and made a slow and careful start on the first craggy chin. No blood, no severed heads, and I became almost competent at shaving. One other strange session was three hours shelling peas into a bucket with a bunch of patients who said nothing in all that time, despite my attempts to get a conversation going.

One night, I was on a late shift and the weather was foul. A storm raged around the hospital. My charge nurse put his phone down and said I needed to go and help remove a dead body from a ward in the women's section of the hospital. I would meet another assistant and between us we would trolley the lady who had died from the ward to the mortuary.

This assignment had all the makings of a horror film. Once let out from the men's section of the hospital, the doors were locked behind me and I spent many minutes in the pouring rain trying to find a way into the women's section. Eventually, I attracted some attention by banging on a ward window, and a nurse came and unlocked a door and let me in. Up I went to the floor where the ward was. There were screams coming from some of the wards and I tried hard not to be distracted from what I was doing.

I found the ward, was let in, and there was the other nursing assistant with this metal box on wheels. Two nurses came and placed the body gently into the box. We closed the lid and left the ward on our way to the mortuary. Again, we had to fight our way out of the locked building. This was in the days before doors with automatically operated locks. Out in the courtyard the rain was still falling in sheets. We found the mortuary and wheeled the trolley in. Before we put her in the freezer, I looked at this little old lady, so peaceful in death. She may have been forced to spend most of her life at St John's because of having an illegitimate child.

Into my mind surged the conviction that this could not be the end of everything for her. A life so apparently condemned to meaninglessness just wasn't possible, I thought. There had to be more to creation than ending up in a freezer in a mental hospital mortuary. As we closed the freezer door, I said goodbye and thank you to this little dead stranger for convincing me that death was not the last word and that therefore there was hope and possibility beyond this life. It was a shot in the arm for what I believed, worth any number of theological essays and lectures.

I still think of that little old lady in the mortuary. I think of all those patients being given large doses of Largactil to keep them under and out of it. And I think of how such efforts were made to close these enormous Victorian asylums and move to care in the community. I believe mental health is still the poor relation where resources and staffing and budgets are concerned. Shame on successive governments.

While at Lincoln I took thirteen GOE – General Ordination Examinations or God's Own Exams. I passed them all and was ready to leave in time to be ordained at Peter-tide at the end of June, or at Michaelmas, at the end of September 1966. It had been decided that Annette and I would work in Somerset where the priest who married us, Michael Percival Smith, was vicar of St John the Baptist, Yeovil. He had shown an interest in having me as one of his curates, so we had travelled down to Somerset in our Austin 7 Chummy – an epic journey as it was snowing and there were over 200 miles to drive. At one point, I had to hammer in the front axle kingpins with a large heavy hammer. I missed and hit my thumb and in the freezing cold, the skin split and blood poured from the wound. I bandaged it up and we continued our journey, kept warm by the engine's heat.

Before I could be ordained deacon, I was asked to produce evidence that I had been baptised. I wrote to the priest responsible for Much Dewchurch, Herefordshire, and with fabulous efficiency, a copy of my baptism certificate arrived almost by return post.

I was required as a matter of courtesy to write to my sponsoring bishop, John Taylor Hughes of Croydon, for permission to leave the college and venture into a parish. He wrote back to say that as I was a nongraduate, I should stay at Lincoln for three years. I replied that there was not a three-year course at Lincoln. Did he really want me to sit through the first year of the course again? He said he was prepared to compromise and that I should stay in college for just three more months, do some reading, and be ordained at Advent. There did not seem to be any point in further argument, and it was fun to be able to read some books that were not about theology, church history, and doctrine.

It might, however, be worth considering what I made of theological education. I believe I was extremely fortunate to have been welcomed to Lincoln Theological College. At least they welcomed the notion and challenges of married students and did what they could to make the tuition interesting. Whether all those lectures, all those examinations, those essays and assignments were worth all the effort and energy and time expended on them, I doubt. But that may be my unretentive brain talking. I would guess that most ministry demands more practical common sense and an ability to listen and talk to people, good communication skills rather than all the academic diet we were fed.

Maybe what was good was learning to rub along with people of very different backgrounds and theological convictions. But I had already absorbed some of that experience working at sea. Yes, parish challenges were as different as they could be from New Testament Greek and Church History. Many people now prepare for ordination at evening and weekend courses, which, I imagine costs less, and may be more helpful before people move on to become deacons and priests. The word 'escape' figures in the next chapter heading but maybe it wasn't so much an escape into a parish as a near drowning in the reality of ministry.

CHAPTER 7

Escape to a parish, or drowning in ministry

Annette and I moved to 50 Grove Avenue, Yeovil, where we shared a parish house with the curate for St Peter's, Westfield, Martin Francis. The other curate, David Nye, looked after St James, Preston Plucknett, a brilliant name. In December I was whisked off to the diocesan retreat house at Glastonbury for the Advent ordination retreat. There was just one other ordinand who was to be a curate at St James' Church, Taunton where the ordination was scheduled for Sunday, 18 December 1966.

During this retreat, there was snow on the ground in Glastonbury. I was walking in the garden of the retreat house, probably terrified at what was about to happen to me. Suddenly, clear as a bell, I heard God asking me, 'What do you want, Patrick?' I looked around but no-one else was in the garden. Without a moment's hesitation, I answered God. 'A child,' I said. And that was that. Nine months later, our son Stephen was born in Yeovil Maternity Unit.

The ordination passed off with little fuss, with just the two of us deacons being ordained by the Bishop of Bath and Wells, Edward Henderson. I discovered later that years earlier he had confirmed my sister Liz. In a few days I was learning how to administer the chalice at a Communion service in St John's Church in Yeovil. Christmas Eve came and with it, my first midnight communion, to which large numbers came. Because of the attendance figures, Michael Smith and I were using some very large, deep chalices. Many of the ladies' hats were of such a size that it was impossible to see exactly what was happening beneath them. I was being very careful not to tip the contents all over them while keeping a close hold on the chalice. As Michael passed me

St John the Baptist, Yeovil

going to and fro, he whispered, 'Patrick, hurry up, we haven't got all night!' I did my best, no wine was spilt, no lady drowned.

Nothing much at theological college prepared me for the shock of working as a curate in a parish. I don't complain, rather I ask, how could it? At college we lived in community, taking meals together, studying and praying and learning together. Suddenly, college is over, exams done, a bishop lays his hands on you, you give general assent to the Thirty-nine Articles of Religion, swear an oath of allegiance to Her Majesty the Queen, and an oath of canonical obedience to your diocesan bishop and his successors in all things lawful and honest, then you are let loose. God help you and the people of the parish.

In a parish there is an amazing amount of stuff to take in very quickly, to do with worship, local custom and practice, the unpredictability of being almost in charge of the church youth club, something I very much doubt I was either equipped or fitted for, but which, as junior curate I was given to do.

There was already a youth leader, Roger, who lost no opportunity to suggest to me that I only worked one day a week. I was silly enough to ignore this for about a year and a half. One day I said very tersely in as threatening a tone as I could muster, 'Roger, if you say that just one more time, I will not answer for my actions.' It must have worked as he never did refer to one day a week again. The reverend worm should have turned much earlier.

When we lived in Upper Norwood, Michael Smith had asked Annette and me to join a team of parish visitors. We were given several houses and flats to visit on behalf of the church. People generally seemed welcoming if slightly pleased or puzzled to be visited. Among the people we visited was a Jewish household. I knew it was because of the mezuzah containing a tiny fragment of the Jewish law placed on the doorpost. We were invited in and made very welcome. I was asked if I knew what the mezuzah was, and I said that I did. In Yeovil visiting members of the congregations as an ordained minister was something entirely new and odd. Wearing my dog collar, I would knock at a door, and be ushered into the coldest room in the house, the front room that had not been used or warmed since Uncle Roderick had been laid out there before his funeral. I found people behaved in a very strange way. I estimate that for a while every such first visit was wasted getting past the weird curate-on-a-pedestal nonsense.

With some households, I used to time my visits to when I thought they might have finished a meal. Then I could ignore the offer of the cold front room and make straight for the kitchen where I might join in the washing up. Timing visits mattered. Targeting the visits mattered too. The vicar would probably know more about the people I was to see, and I never hesitated to ask Michael Smith if there were things I might need to know. I accompanied Michael to one or two funerals before being let loose on my first funeral service. Almost the first question to ask was which undertaker would be handling the situation. Not all undertakers are equal. Some do better than others. In Yeovil, there were two undertakers, Cook and Son, whose funeral director was a Mr Dyer, great name, and the Co-operative Funeral Service. With Cook and Son, you would know if the funeral was high-class or ordinary. Just before the coffin was lowered into the ground, the undertaker would take from a pocket in his tailcoat a wallpaper brush and sweep any pollen from the top of the coffin after the flowers had been removed. For a posh funeral, this brush would be varnished, for a poorer funeral it would be made of plain unvarnished wood. Amazing!

One of my first funerals was that of my father, who died months after slipping and falling on a mainline railway station in London. He fractured his skull and suffered a wandering blood clot in his brain, which meant he couldn't look after himself and suffered huge mood swings. He was looked after at St Bartholomew's Hospital in London, founded by a priest jester, Rahere, in the twelfth century. The hospital kept Dad safe until my mother found him a nursing home in Putney.

I should not have taken my father's funeral, but my mother insisted I should; she could be very forceful, extremely persuasive. I wasn't able to let my grief or feelings mess up the family funeral. And oddly, perhaps, I have learned so much more about my father since his death than ever I knew before he died.

I was required to attend post-ordination training which was generally organised by the then Bishop of Taunton, Frank West. Some sessions were held jointly with newly ordained clergy from the neighbouring Diocese of Bristol. I am not sure what I learned at these sessions except it was good to be away from the demands of the parish, which seemed insatiable. We were made most welcome at the bishop's house in the village of Dinder, where lawns sloped down to a stream and the meals were always delicious.

Yeovil was a town of some 25,000 people. One day I counted the churches and chapels in the town, and I found that there were twenty-one, all needing to be maintained, insured, cleaned. This made me wonder at the sheer choices on offer to the people. It seemed to be mad that there could be so many places of Christian worship in just one town. Indeed, I learned later that one church, a few hundred yards from the parish church of St John the Baptist in the middle of the town, had been built in Victorian times by a splinter group from St John's who thought the worship there was not high enough, Anglo-Catholic enough for their tastes.

At the eight o'clock said Communion service on a Sunday morning, we could tell at St John's whether the priest at Holy Trinity was ahead of us as they rang the church bell during the prayer of consecration. This struck me as completely mad. God knows, any church or chapel costs a fortune to keep open, staffed. In Yeovil I could imagine people in all these religious buildings meeting in their separate boxes wondering if yet another money-raising effort was needed to keep their box open for business. I once counted seven different collecting boxes waiting for their money within just a few feet of a church entrance.

These thoughts surfaced each year during the Week of Prayer for Christian Unity. This was the week when some of us tried hard to forget our historical and doctrinal differences and spend a week loving our fellow Christians of other traditions. One year, the Yeovil clergy had boldly decided to preach in each other's pulpits to show just how united we all were for that week. Alas, when the Roman Catholic bishop of Clifton heard about this revolutionary step, I was told that he wrote to his Roman Catholic clergy in Latin expressly forbidding any such thing to happen. Should not every day be a day of prayer and action for Christian unity, given the scandal of division?

In Yeovil there was a marvellous roadbuilder called Geoff Price who was even more scandalised by the disunity of Christians than I was. Every year he took the lead and organised fundraising for the poor through Christian Aid. For two years I took part in the annual sponsored walk from Wells Cathedral to Yeovil overnight, almost twenty-four miles. On one of these occasions, I was saddened to be required to attend the eight o'clock Sunday morning communion in St John's after arriving absolutely exhausted in Yeovil, having left Wells the previous night. The only way I could keep awake was by constantly moving my head and looking at different parts of the church, which, I hope, puzzled some of members of the congregation.

These walks raised thousands of pounds for the poor and were great experiences. I remember being sent off on the walk by the Bishop of Bath and Wells. Many members of the church youth club took part and two of them spent the whole walk from Wells to Yeovil kicking an aluminium drink can back and forth to each other. I envied their energy.

My vicar, Michael Smith, asked to see sermons I wrote before I delivered them from the pulpit. He would sit and read them while I waited anxiously to hear what he thought or how he suggested I should alter them. Eventually he trusted me to write them and deliver them without him having seen them first.

Preaching is a huge responsibility and anyone who thinks it isn't should probably not be doing it. Too many sermons from newly ordained priests and older priests who ought to know better can be an academic essay read at high speed from the pulpit. The problem with such sermons is that if the listener misses a word or a phrase, that's it, it's gone. Preaching, like radio, is a linear medium, it cannot be re-wound to where it can be read or heard again and maybe understood. Getting and holding the listener's attention is a real challenge, not least because each of them will have pastoral and spiritual needs at that point, which may all be completely different and possibly contradictory. One may be just setting out on their Christian journey; others may be nearing the end of their life. A wise priest, John Barton, told me once that he always tried to include something in his sermons for the person attending church for the very first time, and something for someone whose last visit to a church it might be. Thinking about sermons, it seems to me that God's Holy Spirit will often somehow make a sermon meet the individual and very different needs of the listeners, a theory often borne out by people's reactions afterwards. People often refer to words you can't even remember using. One of the best things anyone said to me after a sermon was to thank me for reminding her that it was alright to be uninhibited in church. She was very old, and it was lovely to hear her interpretation of what I had said and done in the pulpit that morning. Comments are not always that complimentary.

I once had to preach at evensong at St John's Church. It was Bible Sunday and I wanted to leave the congregation in no doubt whatsoever that the Bible is like an explosive, a dangerous book to have in any house. Read and understood, it can and maybe should inspire revolution, turn the world and its values upside down and inside out.

In the days before I was due to preach, I obtained some narrow cardboard tubes, taped them together to look like so many sticks of dynamite. I was able to buy some Jetex fuse from a model shop which sold model aircraft kits. Once in the pulpit, I held up this apparent bomb, and lit the fuse which burned all the way to the supposed sticks of dynamite. I certainly got the attention of the congregation and I hope some of them listened to the end. When I was researching a possible book about preaching, I met someone who said she would never forget the service when the preacher produced a giant cauliflower during his sermon, took a large knife to it and split it in two. For the life of her she couldn't remember the point that was being made, but she would remember the cauliflower till the day she died, she said. Visual aids carry their own dangers, elephant traps for the unwary preacher or listener. Decades later I used one of those candles that refuses to be extinguished as a visual aid in a service being held by a church that met in the local school. A few minutes after I had finished preaching, someone dashed past me to properly extinguish the wicked candle which otherwise might have burnt the school down.

One morning after preaching at matins at St John's Church, I was changing out of cassock and surplice in the vestry where the treasurer was totting up the collection from the service. 'You've preached that sermon before, haven't you,' he said. I replied that if something was worth saying, it would bear repeating. He obviously didn't approve as he said, 'If you go on preaching like that, the numbers will fall and we won't be able to pay you.' I reassured him that in that case I would get a secular job and help the church out at weekends in my spare time. I sensed this wasn't the response he was looking for.

It was not my preaching that got me into trouble at Yeovil but my writing. Colin Morris had written an angry book called *Include Me Out!* which I had read. His writing the book was prompted by an African dropping dead outside his manse in Zambia while Colin was sitting indoors reading the *Methodist Recorder's* account of a serious debate within the Methodist Annual Conference. The question was about whether communion wine should be fermented or not.

A post-mortem revealed that the dead African had just a small ball of grass in his stomach. His possessions were the ragged clothes he was wearing and a broken ball point pen. Colin Morris put these two events alongside each other and wrote his book. Simultaneously another Methodist, Merfyn Temple, was sitting in Westminster Abbey on hunger strike on behalf of the poor and hungry to draw attention to their plight.

In 1968 I wrote a piece about the wealth of the church and the poverty of people and sent it off to *The Western Gazette*, our local paper. The editor said he would not print it as a feature but was prepared to carry it as a reader's letter. I agreed to this, and the roof fell in. People were outraged at what I had written, and there was a meeting of the parochial church council at which, I believe, Michael Smith promised that I would never again do such a thing. It was entirely my mistake and, yes, I should have talked to Michael before writing to the paper and raising such a row. I have heard it said that there is one thing worse than being a curate and that is having one. Never having had a curate, I can still imagine that it would be true.

Interestingly, not all the members of the council were outraged, and I did receive some heartfelt support from members of the congregation at St John's and at the little tin church at the bottom of Grove Avenue, St Andrew's. Looking through the responses to my letter, a former member of the youth club, Michael Whittock, wrote from university in York to support what I had written. He began, 'I am appalled by the shallow thinking and lack of insight which correspondents demonstrated in their replies.' He then went on to argue that there was point and purpose in my original letter. This was a counter to the charge of communism gone mad of which I stood accused at the time.

If nothing else, it brought some life into the Gazette's columns. The paper regularly reported funerals and listed those who had attended them. In later editions, it then strove to correct inaccuracies and apologised for them.

While in Yeovil, I read *New Christian*, a fortnightly paper edited by Trevor Beeson. One day, I found that someone I had known at Lincoln, Richard Kingsbury, had written a comic column. I thought I could have a go at this and submitted a possible article. Trevor Beeson replied that he was happy to publish it and would pay £5 for it. Curiously, the piece appeared, but over Richard Kingsbury's name, which was disappointing for me, surprising for Richard, and embarassing for Trevor Beeson, who apologised. I wrote some more columns and found I could write one in half an hour and get paid £5 which would buy us a week's worth of groceries. Worth doing. Reading them through, my writing comic pieces about the church was helping me to cope with some of the ecclesiastical nonsense I saw around me.

Nine months to the day after God asked me what I wanted and I had replied, 'a child', Annette woke up feeling strange. Because I was away with the youth club, caving in the Mendip Hills, some ten days before the expected birth, Annette was staying with Michael and Elizabeth Smith at the vicarage round the corner in West Park. The tenth of September was a Sunday, it was early, and Annette tried to go back to sleep. She woke again and got up and woke Elizabeth who made a pot of tea. Tea can do all manner of things, but it was not going to stop a child being born and Annette was admitted to the maternity unit, having contractions as she went up in the lift. I was rung at six o'clock and was up, shaved and dressed, and out of the youth centre in ten minutes. I drove across Somerset like Jehu, forty miles in forty minutes. Happily, no police were about, and I arrived at the unit and struggled into a gown and mask in time to see our baby's head appear. Some minutes after the birth, a doctor put his head round the door and asked us what we had. I felt very stupid. We had both been so overwhelmed by the birth and the safe arrival of a child it had not occurred to either of us to see whether it was a boy or a girl. We admitted we did not know, and the doctor looked and told us we had a son. We named him Stephen, as he had undoubtedly been conceived on St Stephen's day, and Robert, after Annette's father. Stephen was clearly in a hurry to be born. The other noteworthy event that September was the opening of BBC Radio 2 which replaced The Light Programme on 30 September. It may become clear why I have mentioned this radio station.

I was ordained priest in St John the Baptist Church, Yeovil on Sunday, 17 December 1967 by the Bishop of Bath and Wells, Edward Henderson. Our priest Michael Percival Smith preached and, according to the local newspaper, called on clergy and congregation alike to go outside the church in search of converts. 'It is no good just sitting in church and waiting for people to come to us,' he said. It was a busy day, ordination in the morning and in the afternoon our son Stephen was baptised by Michael Smith.

CHAPTER 8

A start of sailing

L ife and the church marched on at Yeovil. The Youth Club met in the schoolrooms near the church. It was a handy place for large or small meetings. Upstairs there was a very large hall, and I worked with others to get a grant to build a comfortable and attractive side room in which youth club members could relax and talk. We succeeded with the grant application and the room was built. The county youth service ran courses for youth workers on planning a programme for youth clubs. To be fair, we were never short of ideas for what to do, but it was good to find that other youth leaders and workers were finding teenagers as challenging to deal with, as fickle, as ours were. There were several youth clubs in the town and memberships seemed to be informally interchangeable. We would go to great trouble to organise something the members said they wanted only to find on the day that they had all decided to go somewhere else.

We did try some risky enterprises, with members offering to help pensioners by painting and decorating their homes. We also acquired a chainsaw for cutting up firewood for pensioners. Health and Safety wasn't even a twinkle in the legislators' eyes at that time, thank God.

Another project in which I played some part was the conversion of former Boys' Club premises near the church to be a drop-in centre for people coming into town from the surrounding estates. I remember recommending a system where frozen meals could be bought and stored in large upright freezers, to be defrosted and heated through to provide nourishing meals for pensioners visiting the centre.

Looking back, I can see the development of a sort of ministry of mad ideas in my character and in day-to-day life and work. I love George Bernard Shaw's words, 'You see things; and you say "Why?" But I dream things that never were, and I say, "Why not?"' Put these together with the words of Jesus, 'With God, all things are possible,' and I have an alternative article of faith.

I became involved in writing for a paper called *Contact*, the brain-child of Canon Derek Palmer, a priest in Bristol Diocese. His vision was of a church paper with the outer pages being of regional interest with the inside pages being more local in coverage.

A curacy can be a breathless thing. Work seemed to be incessant. Martha Jacobsen, who had looked after us as children through the war and afterwards into the 1950s, met and married Colonel James Palmer. Years before we moved to Yeovil, they had returned from Singapore and settled in Somerset not far from Yeovil. On days off, we fled to Martha and James' house at Windmill Hill, near Ashill, seventeen miles away. There we could sit and talk, relax, it felt, thousands of miles away from the parish. Martha and James doted on Stephen, with James getting Stephen to run races in their lovely garden.

Once or twice we may have stayed in the house at Grove Avenue on a day off. But it became very clear that no-one else in Yeovil thought we either had a day off or should take one. The only answer was not to be at home. Martin Francis, the curate downstairs, and I bought a second-hand sailing dinghy from a shop in the middle of town. Getting it back to Grove Avenue we set about repairing a large hole in the bottom of the hull. We bought marine plywood, fibreglass, and resin and repaired the hull. Neither of us had any experience of boatbuilding. I suppose I still remembered a bit of boat-handling from my sea-going days, but we were both innocents.

The Eleven Plus model was a heavy, clinker-built boat, and, we found, mostly seaworthy once we had remembered almost too late to replace the plugs in the drain holes at the stern. We would hitch the trailer to our minivan and drive down to Weymouth. Martin and I had some great and scary adventures in that boat. One of these took us far out to sea before we managed to go about and hurtle back to the shore. Lines from the Psalms occurred to us as we struggled not to arrive in France or the Channel Islands. 'All thy storms have gone over me . . . out of the deep have I cried, they reel to and fro and stagger like a drunken man and are at their wits' end.' As we hurtled shoreward we spotted an opening in a harbour wall and shot through into the calm and peace of Portland Harbour. Like drowned rats we squelched up the steps to the yacht club, borrowed their phone, and rang for a taxi to take us back to the beach at Weymouth where Annette and her parents had nearly given up hope of ever seeing us again.

Days off were precious and needed to be defended and maybe we went a bit further than we should have done with that boat, but if nothing else it may have been character-forming and slightly reminiscent of the perils of sailing which the disciples must have known all too well.

One day we had a homeless family arrive on our doorstep. An author, John Robb, and his wife Catherine and their daughter Anna Jane. John was working on a novel about Queen Boudicca's last stand against the Romans. John had written five books, one of which had been made into a film. They stayed with us for around six months. During this time both John and Catherine became ill. The pressure of finishing the book may have contributed. They were eventually admitted to hospital for treatment. The book, *A Season of Chariots*, was published in 1968 by Robert Hale and John sent us a copy.

From reading *New Christian* until it ceased publication, it seemed to me that Southwark Diocese was a place where ideas might just be welcome, where adventurous thinking could be encouraged. I enquired about a possible post in Blackheath based at The Church of the Ascension, whose priest was Paul Oestreicher. That came to nothing and the Bishop of Woolwich, John Robinson, suggested Annette and I go and look at the parish of Kidbrooke. We did, we looked at the church, the parish, and asked about where we might live.

We were shown a poky flat and we asked where our young son Stephen would sleep. 'I think the last man kept his baby in a pram in the hall,' was the answer. This didn't seem a good place for a growing infant to spend his nights. We were not mightily impressed.

CHAPTER 9

To Thamesmead

We rang the Bishop of Woolwich and asked if he had any other vacancies we might consider before travelling back to Somerset. He pointed us to Abbey Wood Estate and Thamesmead. Thamesmead was a massive housing project being designed and built by the Greater London Council in association with the London boroughs of Bexley and Greenwich. It was being built on the Plumstead and Erith marshes, some of which land had been released by the Ministry of Defence from its Woolwich Arsenal estate.

The town was to accommodate some 60,000 people, making a significant contribution to Greater London's housing need. As a site for housing development, the 1,300 or so acres could not have been less promising. Because of the marshy nature of the soil, layers of silty clay and peat above a base of gravel on top of Thanet chalk, absolutely everything had to be piled. An engineer commented, 'To put anything on the bog, you had to either float it on the top and pray, or to put thirty-foot piles underneath.' Even the road drains had to be piled, a situation unique to Thamesmead.

Some thought had been given to building very tall tower blocks, perhaps as tall as thirty storeys. It was found that the air above the development was some of the most polluted air in London. To the east lay Cross Ness Sewage Treatment works, one of the four largest such works in northern Europe. Across the Thames were Beckton Gas Works, Barking Power Station, British Oxygen, and Fords of Dagenham, while to the south there was a lead-smelting works near Abbey Wood Station. This cocktail of horrors, the worst in all of London, hung 150 feet above the ground, so it was decided to limit the tower block height to twelve storeys.

Draining the site was a challenge for the civil engineers. Much of the site was below the high-water mark on the River Thames. Water drained down to the site from the hills and Bostall Heath to the south. The site could only be drained into the Thames during a one-and-a-half-hour period either side of low water. What to do with the surface water outside these times? It was decided to create five balancing lakes and a series of interconnecting canals carrying water no more than two feet deep. Two pumping stations would drain the site into the Thames using huge Archimedean screws. Secondary pumps would be used in more severe conditions. The lakes and four and a half miles of canals not only served the draining and balancing needs of the site but provided amenities for the residents. Such were the civil engineering challenges facing the developers of this 'award-winning town of the 21st century' or 'a million tons of concrete gone wrong', as some people came to describe it.

We moved to 4 Coralline Walk in 1969, among the first twenty families to arrive. The first family, the Goochs lived next door at Number 2. Our maisonette was on the first floor as all accommodation had to be built in the early stage of the development on account of fears about possible flooding. Our move was a bit like landing on the moon without a support system, Annette said. She was right. There were very few facilities in those early days. Doctor Peter Higgins was based in a Portakabin until the health centre was built at Tavy Bridge, the first shopping centre. There was a Community officer employed by GLC Housing, an ex-policeman from Essex, David Llewellyn, who had the unenviable task of answering residents' questions and helping in any way he could as people moved in. He was marvellous at his job.

The majority of those moving to Thamesmead were from the east end of London across the river. There they had lived in comparatively low rent properties, near family and friends, surrounded by street markets. Thamesmead was both a challenge and a shock to many of them. Rents were higher, and in a matter of a few years, rents doubled. Tenants were further away from the support of family and friends and it was difficult and expensive to travel back to see them. Shopping meant crossing the railway line to old Abbey Wood. The development of Thamesmead coincided with anxieties about local unemployment in the area. A petition signed by over 11,704 local people was presented to Parliament in March 1968 protesting the closure of AEI factories in Woolwich by Arnold Weinstock's General Electric Company just when Kidbrooke and Thamesmead estates were being developed. It was said that the closure of these factories and consequent loss of employment led to an increased suicide rate in the area.

The churches were stirred by Bishop John Robinson of Woolwich to work together to plan an ecumenical ministry at Thamesmead rather than rushing in and putting up competing buildings. The Thamesmead Christian Community represented the Church of England, the Roman Catholic Church, the Methodist Church, the Salvation Army, the Congregational and Presbyterian Churches, soon to become the United Reformed Church. The Baptist Church wouldn't join but went ahead and built a large church on Yarnton Way. In those heady days of South Bank religion there were high hopes of churches drawing closer together. Although relationships with the Baptist minister David Manktelow were cordial and friendly, there was little or no contact in pastoral matters. Indeed, one story was that the Baptist message on many a doorstep was, 'Don't have anything to do with the Thamesmead Christian Community – they don't believe in the Bible.' Oh dear, oh dear. And to think that Jesus prayed that his followers might all be one.

I was based initially at William Temple Church on Eynsham Drive on the Abbey Wood estate. When I arrived, the priest in charge was Alan Bradbury. This was technically my second curacy. In those days, two curacies were served before priests were let loose in charge of a parish. Alas, now it is the custom and practice for a single curacy to be served before being handed charge of the cure of souls in a parish. Looking back at the curious legal documents charting my progress on the near horizontal ladder of Anglican ministry, I note that technically

I was a curate from when I was first ordained deacon in St James Church, Taunton in December 1966 until I was appointed as Team Vicar in the Thamesmead Team Ministry in July 1974, the team having come into being on 12 March.

William Temple Church had been built in 1966. It had underfloor heating and windows made with stained glass from a bombed-out church in the Surrey docks. The frame of the church was made of concrete uprights filled in with brickwork. The adjoining single-storey accommodation consisted of a kitchen, a meeting room, and an office for the priest. The meeting room and kitchen were a lifesaver of a café, and a place for young people to gather in the evenings. It was a place where news was shared, where pastoral opportunities were revealed and acted on. The church building had its problems, the floor was cracked, and I believe there was some enquiry by the Archdeacon of Greenwich into the churches designed by this architect. It was, however, light and airy and a world away from Norman, Gothic, and other traditional church styles.

One day a family came into the café in some distress. I was in the office at the time and came out to meet them. The story was that the father had died, the funeral had taken place, but the family was convinced that their dad hadn't left the house. It felt haunted and they were terrified. I listened and said that I would be round to see them within a day or two to sort it out. After they left, I rang Southwark Diocesan Office and talked to the priest in charge of exorcism matters, Canon John Pearce-Higgins. I told him what had happened, and he said in a very matter of fact way that he would put a sheet of directions in the post to me. This duly arrived and I acted on the instructions. I gathered some members of the William Temple congregation and we went to the house and held a simple service of Holy Communion, after which I went and blessed all the doors and windows. The family later reported that all was well and what I had done had effected the change they had been seeking. The easiest and the most wounding response would have been for me to tell them not to be so silly. It may indeed have all been in their mind but was certainly no less real for all that.

A mum on the estate got in touch one day when she was in despair. Her husband was in prison, it was a very hot summer, and her fridge had broken and she couldn't afford to replace it. By some marvellous coincidence the fridge in the church coffee bar was about to be thrown out because there was a split in the plastic food compartment. The unit, however, was perfectly serviceable. I resolved to try a refrigerator unit transplant, and after a lot of puzzling, I managed to remove the faulty unit from her fridge and swap it for the café fridge unit. It worked and I was frankly as surprised as she was. The church café was literally a godsend on that estate.

The church had a lively group of young people who shared an interest in folk music. One of their dads, Ted Sproule, wrote what he called folk dramalogues, a mixture of stories with folk music. We would present these in the church on Sunday evenings. One evening, a group of teenagers knocked on the café door and asked if they could join the church youth club. I explained as gently as I could that it was a church youth club for young people who came to the church. They were not pleased. The next morning, I discovered that before they left they had climbed onto the roof of our Renault 4 and pushed the roof in with their bovver boots by jumping along it, teenage kangaroos.

The contrast between the leafy roads of Yeovil and the streets of the Abbey Wood estate could not have been more extreme, but I felt more at home in South London. The local hospital, St Nicholas Hospital, Plumstead was not big enough to qualify for the appointment of a full-time chaplain, so the wards were split up for the local clergy to visit. I had two wards, one a barrack-shaped men's ward within which around sixteen men gazed at sixteen other fellow patients. The patients were mostly suffering from chest and heart problems and over the years I got to recognize people who returned to the ward. Before every cardiac patient was discharged, they would be sternly lectured by the duty doctor or consultant about the dangers of thinking they were being let loose as good as new. They were warned not to go out and shovel snow off the pavement outside their homes. They were told not to push vehicles in the hope of starting them, and in no circumstances were they ever to work on scaffolding or a roof.

When I saw them return months after leaving hospital, I would make a point of asking what they were doing before being admitted. A good few told me a little shamefacedly that they had been taken ill after clearing snow off the pavement, pushing vehicles in the cold, or working above ground level. Men, I observed, are not good at being ill. While I wouldn't dare to claim that women thrive on being ill, they certainly cope better than men with being in hospital. In fairness, some of this may have been due to the different shapes of the wards I visited. Whereas the men's ward was shaped like a barrack room, women's surgical was cross-shaped with four bays looking to a nurses' station in the middle.

The one person I remember most vividly on this men's ward was my favourite undertaker of all time, Ken Hosegood of the Royal Arsenal Cooperative Funeral Service. He was brilliant at his job, never took families to the cleaners, and was one of the funniest men I have ever met. He and I were once involved with a funeral at Eltham Crematorium, a hugely pressured place. One service running late could prejudice the whole day's service schedule. Ken and I were waiting in the foyer of the chapel, separated from the service in progress by glass doors. I mentioned to him that time was running on, the service was running perilously over time. 'Leave it to me, Patrick,' he said, and broke into a wonderfully music hall, silent dance of time routine. It would have been a hit on YouTube. Only the minister inside the chapel would have seen this silent song and dance through the glass windows. He quickly got the message and curtailed his endless address and brought the service to its conclusion. Ken had saved the day.

One of the more difficult elements of our ministry at Thamesmead was the need every year to form a rota with other clergy who could be available to take funerals at Eltham Crematorium for people who hadn't looked for or couldn't find a minister to take the funeral. I would be there, the hearse would arrive, the limousines would disgorge the mourners, all unknown to me and in a matter of minutes I would be taking this vital service for someone about whom I knew nothing for people I would never see again. I used to dread the arrival of our week for taking these services. I am sure each of us did the very best we could but given the circumstances it could not be a very good best. I sometimes wonder why there were these priest-less arrangements. Were the clergy of Kent not bothered? Could they not find space in their diaries for a distant cremation? Did the undertakers forget to ask for a priest or did the families not want the services of a god-botherer?

One day, while visiting the men's ward in St Nicholas Hospital, I found undertaker Ken Hosegood in one of the beds. Unusually for a chest-and-heart ward, Ken was there having broken an ankle or some other bone after tripping over a kerb. In no time at all, Ken managed to cheer the ward up. He had brought all his funeral promotional literature and his measuring tape with him. As soon as he was up and about, he visited every man in that ward, left them the literature, and measured them up. What a man!

From time to time I would be asked by a mum on the women's ward if I would care to baptise her child. I would always ask where she lived, and if she lived in the parish of St Nicholas, Plumstead, I would explain that much as I would be delighted and honoured to baptise her child, she needed to approach her own parish priest. Alas, that was the death sentence as the priest in those days was a rigorist who insisted that the parents come to his church for six months before he would consider baptising their child. I lost track of how many women found themselves confronted with this set of hurdles. It didn't seem to make any sense to me. I love the story in Acts 8 where the Ethiopian eunuch is riding in his carriage while trying to make sense of the book of the prophet Isaiah. Philip, inspired by the Holy Spirit, is directed to go and help him understand the scripture was speaking of Jesus. They passed a watery place and the eunuch asked to be baptised. He confessed his belief in Jesus, Son of God, and was baptised there and then. So, pray silence for another elephant, one of very many. How do I reconcile the prompting of God's Holy Spirit in a pastoral situation with rule-based religion? How does rigorist ministry help anyone? And are not the occasional offices, services of baptism, marriage, funerals such promising opportunities for ministry and pastoral care, surely not to be lightly thrown away?

There was a knock on our door on Coralline Walk. Outside was a mum from the Abbey Wood Estate. She asked if I was the vicar and I explained that I was the curate. 'How soon could you baptise my five children?' she asked. 'What's the rush?' I asked. 'My mother-in-law has baked a nice cake and wants the children to be done.' I said that if it was a good cake it would keep and that I would come and visit her to discuss the matter. A few days later I went to meet her and the children at their home on Sewell Road. I said that I would be happy to baptise her five children if that was what she really wanted me to do. Her mother-in-law not being there, she felt free enough to say that baptism was the last thing she wanted. Her mother-in-law had said that if the children were not baptised and died through, for example, falling into the fire, they would go straight to hell. I explained that God was not such a monster, and that if she didn't want her children baptised, so be it, but if she did we could talk about what God was really like and what baptism meant, and all would be well. My good friend David Matthiae, who worked with me to build television sets while we were students at Lincoln, once said to me that he believed people were loved into the kingdom of heaven, not scared or terrified out of their wits into belonging.

Tony Castle was the Roman Catholic curate for the parish of Abbey Wood. One year he organised a sponsored walk for youth club members for Christian Aid, to buy a bull or a cow for an Indian village, I think. The distance was thirty miles. He oversaw map reading. The walk started in Abbey Wood and wound its way into North Kent, and then back to Abbey Wood. I took part and by the end my knees were beginning to hurt a great deal. Unfortunately, the last mile or so was down a steep hill to Abbey Wood from Bostall Woods. The hill was appropriately enough called Knee Hill. After we got to the bottom and were trying to recover, we discovered that Tony had made a bit of a mistake with the map reading and that we had all walked thirty-one miles. Years later Tony Castle left the priesthood to marry and worked at writing and publishing. What a staggering loss to the ordained ministry! And, I imagine, all because of a rule in his church that priests must be celibate. At this point I always think of the story of Jesus healing Peter the Apostle's mother-in-law. Presumably Peter, the foot-in-mouth rock on which Jesus built his church, was married, so where on earth does all this enforced celibacy stuff come from and does it help?

When women were ordained to the Anglican priesthood, several priests said goodbye to the Church of England and were welcomed into the Roman Catholic Church, even though they were married. I believe we waved them goodbye with a grant to help them settle into their new church. I am told that some of them, finding the Roman Catholic Church not quite the heaven they thought it might be, returned to the Anglican fold. I have also been told that they kept their grant for leaving in the first place. A gigantic Roman Catholic elephant in the room. The Pope is said to be considering whether married priests can serve remote parishes in South America. I suspect they have been doing so for years.

The Anglican priest at William Temple Church, Alan Bradbury, left and was replaced eventually by John Colchester. A prospective team leader was needed for the Thamesmead group. I remember clergy meetings at which the qualities of whoever was appointed should be expected to have were discussed at enormous length. He must be good at worship, at visiting, a team player, on and on it went, line after line of hoped for qualities. I remember becoming exasperated and saying aloud that we should save time and just advertise for God and be done with it. Jim Thompson, a former chartered accountant, who had trained at Cuddesdon, came to Thamesmead with his wife Sally and their two children Ben and Anna. The original Thamesmead clergy team consisted of Jim Thompson, Frank O'Sullivan the Roman Catholic priest, Methodist minister David Ray, United Reformed Church Industrial Chaplain Paul Fuller, and me. One crucial appointment in 1969 to the team was that of Claire Chisholm as pastoral social worker. There was so much need at Thamesmead and Claire was a key worker across the whole community. When she left in 1972 Thamesmead and the team lost a great resource and a good friend. The Bishop of Woolwich, John Robinson, who had suggested that Annette and I look at working at Thamesmead and Abbey Wood Estate, left Woolwich to be Dean of Trinity College, Cambridge in 1969 after ten years as bishop. He was succeeded by former England cricketer David Sheppard who had been working at The Mayflower Centre in London's East End.

In the early Thamesmead years, we met for services on Sunday morning in an old people's clubroom, Evenlode House, adjoining Coralline Walk. Jim Thompson looked back fondly on those early services, with all the stuff needed for a Communion service carried to the venue in two supermarket carrier bags. I remember vividly a baptism service held on Easter Eve. The clubroom was packed and at one point someone's bouffant hairstyle caught fire and she had to be extinguished with some water from the kitchen, almost strikingly New Testament!

I was torn in two by the demands and needs of the Abbey Wood Estate and William Temple Church and the growing challenge of Thamesmead as it began to welcome increasing numbers of incomers from all over London.

Once John Colchester arrived at William Temple Church, I was free to work exclusively at Thamesmead. There was so much to do, the needs were so many and pressing. One of the obvious gaps in the mix was a regular newssheet for people as they arrived and settled in. In December of 1969 I started a grisly duplicated sheet called *Mesmedaath*, not the most striking of titles but as you will have spotted it was an anagram of Thamesmead. In this I put absolutely everything that might be of use or interest to the newcomers. It helped that Annette, Stephen, and I were newcomers too. We were most definitely all in the same boat. It was not a parish magazine. I had heard by then of a celebrated parish priest who said that whenever he saw a parish magazine, he would tear it up because of the harm that it might do. A bit strong perhaps but some parish magazines can seem quite odd and strange as I discovered when we left Thamesmead to work in the Diocese of St Albans.

Mesmedaath was appallingly titled, looked like a duplicated dog's dinner and probably no-one mourned its passing less than I did. The *Kentish Independent* offered to produce its successor, *Insight*. I was the editor, and the publishers were the Thamesmead Community Association of which I was a founder member. The first edition appeared in May 1970. It had pictures. The lead story was about the dangers of children playing unsupervised on the site, which was the largest adventure playground in the world. It was written by the site safety officer Kevin Cullen. It told of two children aged three and six years old who had been rescued from the third floor at Block 13, the bit that juts into Harrow Manorway. The six-year-old said, 'We were playing. It was fun.' Two youngsters, three and four years old, were rescued from the ninth floor of a tower block being built. They had been happily sitting on the hoist run. 'A great machine,' they commented. An eight-year-old 'was climbing up the scaffolding trying to perform the Indian rope trick and vanish into thin air.' He was thirty feet above ground level. Kevin Cullen reminded parents that they were responsible for their children. On the back page, our son Stephen appeared, aged just two and a half years. The story was that he was looking forward to some designated play space near Coralline Walk. The GLC had promised to investigate this question five months earlier but there was no news. There is a note to say that there were still no shops some eighteen months into the development. Of course, traders would want a significant number of potential customers before risking opening a new venture at the first designated local centre, Tavy Bridge. Finally, the long wait ended and the first shop opened on Tavy Bridge. What was it? A betting shop, the very last thing we needed there and then.

In the same edition a German visitor to the Thamesmead clergy group, Pastor Helga Trösken, commented that 'colours have not been planned for Thamesmead. Could it be that the GLC planners never have to live here? People don't have to walk around Thamesmead – they can be blown around. Hats off to the planners, so to speak!' There was a story of GLC officers being shown around a new housing development in Iceland where a riot of colours characterised the estate. One was heard to say to another, 'We're not having that at Thamesmead.' They didn't live at Thamesmead.

One of the early arguments I remember from those early days at Thamesmead was with my fellow members of the Thamesmead Community Association Committee. They held that *Insight* should only be delivered to residents who had joined the Association, the TCA. As editor, and I hoped, the only likely editor for the time being, I protested that it would be much easier if *Insight* was delivered to everyone without exception. Imagine walking along an elevated walkway in the rain at night, trying to discern by torchlight who were members and who were not. Besides, I added, advertisers would want to know there was 100 per cent coverage. And how else would people learn about the TCA and its activities on their behalf if they didn't receive *Insight*? With any luck this was the clincher and the question never arose again while I was editor.

Some months later the *Kentish Independent* stopped producing *Insight*. One story was that one of the directors urgently needed a cricket club programme to be printed. He was unable to have it when he wanted because *Insight* was taking up the printing facility. The TCA then took the publication in-house and I worked with a small team to produce it every month. We were greatly blessed with Adrian Barnard who was a graphic designer working in advertising. We set to with Letraset for headlines and subheading, and I quickly learned how to mark-up pictures so that they could fit in the appropriate spaces.

Sticking down the Letraset was done with a powerful adhesive called Cow Gum. Was it really made from rendered-down cows, I wondered? Whether it was or not, it was a powerful and smelly adhesive. I'm surprised we didn't become ill or addicted, snorting flame from our nostrils, all dragon-like. The typesetting of the copy was farmed out to the printers, Brewsters of Rochester. Once we had the paste-up completed, usually around midnight, I would drive it down to the printers in Gas House Road, Rochester, just across the Medway Bridge. I was once stopped by the police who wanted to know what I was doing so late in Rochester. I told them that I edited Thamesmead's *Insight* and had just popped the paste-up through Brewsters' door in Gas House Road. It was probably sufficiently unlikely to be untrue, so they let me return to Thamesmead.

I edited *Insight* until we left Thamesmead in 1978. It then continued until 1987 when it was replaced by a paper called *Thamesmead Times* produced by Thamesmead Town Ltd until 1994. We realized that we could save money every month and save time in the process if we brought the typesetting in house. We bought a second-hand Addressograph/Multigraph typesetting machine which we paid for over a year or two. Copy was typed into the machine twice, emerging as justified columns to our specification. After some years out, I was in the communications business again.

We only ever had one near miss in terms of the law and *Insight*. Adrian Barnard was the assistant editor as well as designer. One year, Annette, Stephen, and I went on holiday and left him in charge. When we returned, we found that I was about to be sued as editor. Perhaps the TCA as publisher was under threat as well. Adrian had begun to write a monthly column which took a mostly humorous look at things Thamesmead. The column was headed 'Six of One'. In the edition in question, he had wondered in print whether one of the shops, the fish bar, would open on Town Show day as it had done the previous year. Shops usually stayed closed on Town Show day as the show's purpose was to give the people of Thamesmead and the surrounding area a great day out while raising funds for all the good causes and projects on the development. Adrian finished his piece by writing that if the fish shop did open on that day, he was sure our readers would know what to do. Technically, I was told, this constituted a libellous threat to the fish bar's trade. Distraint of trade, I think, was the legal phrase. Happily, the TCA Committee talked the proprietor out of his promised lawsuit, perhaps with the possibility of his being barred from their licensed premises. He backed off and a great sigh of relief was heard from the next meeting of the editorial group in Adrian and Heather Barnard's flat in Blewbury House.

As I have mentioned the Town Show, this was an idea that arose from the conviction that as Thamesmead had no traditions or history as a housing development, we had better start some traditions to help people feel a sense of place and community. Bexley Borough Council, said by some to be the meanest of all the London boroughs, and staunchly Conservative too, wrote to us one year and asked if we could call the day by some other name, because, they said, they wanted us to feel part of Bexley community. We said no, as I don't think anyone at Thamesmead felt that Bexley cared very much about Thamesmead at all. For example, when the first library was opened in the Bexley third of Thamesmead, we learned that the only reason that there were any books in the library was because all the other Bexley libraries had offered to forego their annual allocation of books so that Thamesmead's library could have any books at all. Parkway, the second Bexley Primary School in Thamesmead was only half built, in modern construction, as Bexley believed there would never be enough children to warrant the completion of the plans. So, our son Stephen spent much of his time at Parkway School being taught in Portakabins.

This political division of Thamesmead was one of the complicating factors in the development. Two thirds of Thamesmead were within the Inner London borough of Greenwich, the balance being in Bexley borough's area. This meant that schools were divided between the Inner London Education Authority, under the Greater London Council, while the balance were the responsibility of Bexley Borough Council. The developer of the site was the Greater London Council, whose political colour changed every four to five years, while Greenwich was solidly Labour and Bexley remained Conservative, although the Bexley part of Thamesmead fell within the parliamentary constituency of Erith and Crayford, well served by Labour Member of Parliament James Wellbeloved.

All this complexity meant that Thamesmead, for which there were new town hopes and ambitions, could not be a new town within the meaning of the act. Consequently, there was no access to funding or planning from the New Towns Development Corporation. Thamesmead matters were time and again political footballs to be played with various degrees of interest and skill and consequent delays between the two boroughs – one Inner London, one Outer London – and the Greater London Council. Negotiating with the boroughs and the Greater London Council could be and often was nightmarish. Had we been a proper new town like Milton Keynes, Basildon, or Harlow, all manner of questions might have been dealt with less slowly and with less complexity. It was a struggle sometimes to know to whom we should be writing or talking. I think it would be fair to say that we had very good relationships with the Thamesmead architects and the Thamesmead manager, architect Geoffrey Horsfall, while we found the GLC Housing Department to be much more of a challenge. Much later in our time at Thamesmead, two of us were co-opted to the Thamesmead committee of the Greater London Council at County Hall. Architect Peter Goodwin, a member of the Church of the Cross, and I spent many bewildering hours in committee meetings trying to put across the views of the residents.

At least, thank God, Thamesmead fell within the Anglican Diocese of Southwark and lines of communication were kept straightforward and clear. We felt there was a commitment, largely pioneered by Bishop John Robinson, and taken on by Bishop David Sheppard. As we tried to establish ways of working and being appropriate to the mostly ecumenical approach taken by the churches involved in the Thamesmead Christian Community, we tried to learn by seeing how other pastoral provision was working. We certainly went to look at Roundshaw, a housing development being built near Croydon.

At some point we discussed as a team what the church should be about in this place of no history. We concluded that the church had two parallel aims, to share the gospel of Jesus Christ and to serve the community without strings attached. I am sure our original statement was a bit longer, something to do with building groups to stand for the reality of God. Editing always improves matters. It was an early mission statement rather than a deadly assumption like 'well, we all know what we are doing here, don't we?'

We endlessly discussed the pros and cons of building a church. We had become used to meeting in community rooms for worship, but the question of a building would not go away. In the end I think we voted equally both for and against a building, but a casting vote set us on the path of trying to design a building that would work round the clock seven days a week and twenty-four hours a day. The Church of the Cross was built at the end of Lensbury Way. It was designed by architect Charles Brown. It had a budget of some £53,000. Given that the building had to be built on piles into the boggy ground, I think we got a good deal for our money. There was a large worship area which had movable screens which meant it could be divided into three sections for different activities. There was a kitchen with a serving hatch into the main worship area. There was a meeting room, and an office as well as lavatories and washrooms. It was single storey and, I think, it worked very well. It was opened in July 1973, soon after the Baptist Church in Yarnton Way which opened in February.

There was a great service to mark the opening. Annette with others, including the Methodist minister's wife Susan Ray and Eric Shegog's wife Ann, had formed a liturgical dance group. It was much helped and inspired by the work of a group led by Margaret Stephens based at the Church of the Ascension, Blackheath. The Church of the Cross group choreographed an offertory dance for the service. Something went a touch amiss and the bread wasn't collected and the Bishop of Southwark, Mervyn Stockwood, stage-whispered, 'Where's the bread?' Unabashed the dancers circled again, this time picking up the bread and delivering it to the bishop. Very Anglican.

After the service was over, we locked up the building and went home. We woke the next day to discover that the Church of the Cross had been broken into and over £1,000 worth of video equipment had been stolen among other items. The video gear belonging to Greenwich Cablevision who had been filming the service was, we discovered, insured. Outraged residents remarked to Jim Thompson that it was disgraceful that the church had been burgled. He replied that everyone else was being burgled, why should the church expect to escape?

While discussing the design of the building, the question of whether we should buy a church organ came up. On balance we decided not to. We had an eclectic group of musicians within the congregation. David Lowrence was a Morris dancer and played the accordion. His wife, Elaine, played the oboe. I sort of played the twelve-string guitar. Val Gibson played the guitar. Margaret Booth played the clarinet, and her husband Martin played the violin. A couple of children played recorders. We did acquire a piano from somewhere and a Methodist played this.

The Church of the Cross was, without doubt, a valuable community building. In no time at all, there were weight-watcher groups, martial arts, Brownies, and a playgroup meeting there.

Annette's father Robert Miller offered to paint a triptych for the church. The church was delighted to accept, and he started work on a brilliant work of art which eventually was hung on the brick wall behind where the altar used to be placed facing the doors. The central panel showed Jesus on the Cross while the side panels displayed the bread and wine.

The painting took him months to do. Thinking about it and painting it led Robert to ask his local parish priest to prepare him for confirmation. He painted it in a studio shed in the garden of their home in Lower

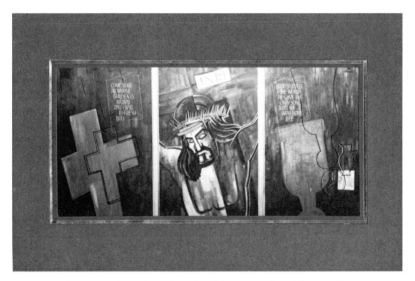

The triptych at The Church of the Cross by Robert Miller

Willingdon, outside Eastbourne. The painting lifted the inside of the Church and gave the space a focus and a reference. Outside the front door of the church stands an enormous wooden cross.

My work at Yeovil with the project to establish a drop-in centre where pensioners could get an affordable nutritious meal had probably prepared me for my role at Thamesmead which eventually became formalised as Team Vicar with responsibility for community development – a bit of a mouthful if ever there was. I was a founder member of the Thamesmead Community Association and the editor of *Insight*. Additional roles emerged with a sort of chaplaincy with the Bexley Social Work team and with the Lakeside Health Centre at Tavy Bridge. It mattered that there was support for the teams working all the hours with individuals and families coming to live there. It mattered too that there was grassroots feedback to the authorities regarding the consequences of their planning and other decisions.

Thamesmead, being virgin territory, was the target for every possible sales representative. I imagined regional sales meetings in which Thamesmead was printed in red on sales maps and representatives were urged to get in there and make a killing. We were bombarded by literature encouraging us to buy a chest freezer already stuffed with frozen meat. Already faced with the pressures of moving into a bright new dwelling, suddenly it was easy to agree with salespeople that maybe it was time to replace the cheap and cheerful and maybe tired furniture with something bright and new and easily affordable on hire purchase. Many families were encouraged to spend beyond their means and as a result got into financial difficulties.

An extreme example for us was the occasion when a salesman knocked at our door on Coralline Walk and spent maybe twenty minutes failing to convince me that I should buy a first aid kit from him, costing just thirty shillings, and yes I could have it for just one shilling a week! I said time and again that I did not want to buy his first aid kit, and he became more and more exasperated. Finally, he asked why. I pointed across the walkway and said, 'that's where my GP, Doctor Schilling lives.' A weak excuse but I didn't know what else to say.

One of the early pressing problems was the incidence of rain penetration into the flats and maisonettes built using the Balency system of house construction. I was told that there was such a shortage of building trades people – bricklayers, carpenters – that the government was encouraging local authorities to employ industrial methods to produce housing units. The housing factory was built on the site and huge concrete components were made there and then conveyed to where they were needed on site. One of the consequences of using concrete for walls was the near impossibility of drilling into them to hang shelves or pictures. I think the tenancy agreement prohibited unauthorised drilling into these wall panels, not only because it was nearly impossible to do without an impact drill and a diamond tipped drill bit, but because in certain sections the concrete concealed water pipes and electrical cables, which would be difficult to reroute if they became damaged.

We discovered that out of the first 1,300 dwellings to be occupied, about a third of them leaked when it rained. While some people were outraged and severely inconvenienced by this rain penetration, not everyone complained. David Llewellyn told me once that he had visited an eighty-year-old pensioner in his nice new flat. He asked the newcomer how he had settled in. The pensioner was grateful to the point of embarrassment and it took a very determined David to get him to admit that, yes, when he switched one of his room lights on, he was a little concerned at the water dripping from the light fitting.

The Greater London Council did not cover itself with glory in its response to this crisis in its award-winning 'town of the 21st century'. They insisted that any mould in the houses, flats, or maisonettes was due to inadequate ventilation. Tenants should make sure that windows were kept open. Repeated complaints to the GLC were either ignored or brushed off. I think I upset the chairman of the Thamesmead committee, Mr Seton Forbes-Cockell, no relation, by sending him a telegram insisting that my GP Doctor Schilling knew the difference between mould caused by lack of ventilation and damp caused by rain penetration. Meetings with senior officials became more fraught with both GLC representatives and TCA officers refusing to accept a common note of the proceedings. Eventually the TCA told the GLC that it was prepared and could afford to take the GLC to court on the grounds that it was not providing housing to the standard required under one or other of the housing acts. Even this move failed to produce any admission of a problem or urgent search for a remedy.

Finally, we hit on a game changer. We had huge posters printed with the legend I'VE GOT DAMP printed in bold red capitals and overnight delivered them to every occupied dwelling on the site with a covering letter asking that if the resident experienced rain penetration, they should exhibit the poster in the most visible of their windows. Within hours a rash of these posters appeared all over the development. And within hours, official visitors on GLC guided tours were asking embarrassing questions about the meaning of these posters. Because of the apparently random distribution of the posters, it was not possible to guarantee that any visitor's route would be free from them.

Within twenty-four hours, a maisonette had been commandeered by the GLC and a team of scientists and engineers were quartered there to begin to sort out the problem. As we suspected, the cause was not the feckless resident who refused to have polar draughts roaring through his house. One story was of a white-coated scientist practically in tears saying that he had never seen rain falling upwards before. This was probably due to the winds around the tower blocks causing vortices which drew rain upwards. Rain should behave better. It didn't happen on the French Riviera or in Ireland where the Balency system had been used. An associated cause, we were told, may have been that the mastic jointing in between the huge external concrete panels was squeezed into the miles of joints with the operatives being paid more the faster they applied the mastic.

I am sure that GLC probably cursed the day they helped the TCA to form, so much of a nuisance did we cause them over this and other matters. It mattered though that good communications were maintained as far as possible. It mattered too that while we needed to try to solve problems, we also worked hard at making things work, got positive projects off the ground. Jim Thompson's wife Sally was much involved in the work to get playgroups in place for all the children who moved to Thamesmead or were born there.

We helped to form the Thamesmead Community Workers Group, certain that professionals across all the disciplines needed to work together across disciplinary boundaries, to identify areas of need and plan how best to mobilise support and problem solving. The group met regularly at the Lakeside Health Centre.

The clergy team soon realised that they would have to work on their own pastoral care. No-one from beyond the estate was going to step in and wag fingers and say 'enough' if we got stressed. We shared reading days when we would leave the estate and book a room at a Roman Catholic convent school for the day. We would read in silence whatever book we liked, and only talk and discuss during coffee and tea breaks or over a delicious lunch prepared by the Methodist cook.

Once a year we booked three days at the Friars at Aylesford for the clergy team. We went with no agenda, and relaxed and shared whatever was on our minds. We joined the Carmelite community for their services, went for long walks, and enjoyed the meals often finishing up in the village pub. We also picked delicious blackberries from the village hedgerows.

Some six or seven years into Thamesmead, we suggested a similar de-stressing break for the general practice team. They laughed and said they couldn't possibly leave the practice for a day or three . . . people would die. We persevered and eventually they set up an away trip to Aylesford. They warned the Thamesmead community of the emergencies-only period at the Health Centre through *Insight* and arranged for a consultant to handle real emergencies. I went with them as chaplain, and it soon became clear that the visit wouldn't work – they had some seven years of piled-up issues to deal with. At least that was my interpretation. By the end I hope they had at least identified areas of their work which needed attention. When they returned to Thamesmead and the Health Centre they found perhaps to their surprise and relief that the population had indeed survived their absence. No-one had died.

One of the issues we found within the Community Workers Group was the incidence of marital breakdown at Thamesmead. There was all manner of contributory causes, new town blues, financial problems, relationship issues, isolation, depression. To some extent we all seemed to be picking up on this, teachers, police, youth workers, social services, clergy. New town blues was a new concept to all of us. All in our different ways were involved. Marriage Guidance, locally based in Bexleyheath, two bus rides away, had a three-month waiting list to be seen. This was, we thought, far too long a wait, never mind the travelling. We decided to set up a project to help with this challenge. We called it MASH – Marriage and Self Help. We asked Marriage Guidance if they could help us with some training. Their answer was short and to the point. We shouldn't be doing this work, they said, because we were not trained. They would not help. So, we did the best we could. I went on a course to do with conjoint family therapy according to the model of Virginia Satyr, led by a psychiatrist, Doctor Rena Proud.

Couples were seen by appointment at the Lakeside Health Centre. At the first meeting we asked that both people came to an agreed number of sessions together. Between us we did the very best we could to help heal relationships which were under immense strain in the development.

CHAPTER 10

More Thamesmead

One of my ways of coping with the stress of working at Thamesmead was to sign up for a course to take my mind off all things church. The first one was at Morley College where I studied a year's course on Neighbourhood and Community led by Clifford Wright. When this was completed, Annette and I both signed on to study for a London University diploma in sociology taught over four years at Goldsmith's College.

Sociology, my brother Mike told me, is the study of those who don't need studying by those who do. I found it mostly fascinating. Annette left the course but one day woke up to say she was tired of doing secretarial work. She said she would like to train as a teacher. She found a part-time course designed for students who were mothers with school-age children. It was a four-year course based at Rachel McMillan College of Education in the New Kent Road near the Elephant and Castle.

By this time, we were living in our own little house in Plumstead, Southeast London, literally just up the road from Thamesmead. For the first two to three years, we lived at 4 Coralline Walk, Thamesmead, and were very happy there. We did find the fact that Thamesmead had won an international planning award came with its disadvantages. Thamesmead was rarely out of the news. People who lived in other areas covered by our local newspapers must have got fed up to the back teeth with this troublesome development on the banks of the Thames. By the time we left for St Albans Diocese in 1978, the population of Thamesmead at some 17,000 people had exceeded the number of official visitors to the site. There were visits by groups of Japanese architects, United States senators, town planners, and architects from around the world. At one point there was serious discussion about putting up signs saying that real people lived at Thamesmead. It was not a zoo, though from time to time people felt that that was exactly what Thamesmead was. One lunch time we came down from upstairs to find that a party of official Japanese tourists had entered the maisonette. Yes, we had the front door open to allow air to move through the rooms.

When Jim and Sally Thompson came to Thamesmead, life got a bit easier. Before he had been ordained Jim had qualified and worked as an accountant. Jim was chaplain at Cuddesdon Theological College; Sally is a historian. They had two children, Ben and Anna, and they moved into 7 Wolvercote Road, about five minutes' walk from Coralline Walk where we lived.

My work was morphing from traditional house-to-house visiting on the Abbey Wood estate and the beginning of Thamesmead into something around community development. John Colchester was appointed to William Temple Church, Abbey Wood Estate in 1971. The needs of Thamesmead were infinite, there being no history, no tradition. Everything had to be invented, brand new from scratch.

Ordained clergy are expected and, in many cases, required to live over the shop, in the parish. It was agreed in 1971 that we could instead be paid a housing allowance of £26.66 a month, the rental for 4 Coralline Walk, and with this we bought a tiny house on the edge of Plumstead Common, 121 Roydene Road. It was priced at just £3,900. When we agreed to buy it, the estate agent in Bexleyheath asked us for a deposit and how much would I like to put down. I said, '£10.' He didn't bat an eyelid at this tiny sum, and the deal was done. I plead ignorance. Nobody ever told me that the usual deposit was around 10 per cent of the purchase price. While negotiations, surveys, and the legal business progressed, the house was broken into and vandalised. All the plumbing, including lead piping, was stripped out and most of the windows were smashed. We went back to the estate agents and said we were not prepared to pay the original amount given all the repair work that needed to be done. The estate agent revised the price downwards, £3,700 if they did the repairs, £3,300 if we did. We settled on the lower figure and I quickly learned the basics of plumbing and glazing. There was a nasty moment when we received a letter from the Greater London Council whom our solicitors had been instructed to write to accept their offer of a mortgage on the Plumstead house. The letter said that the offer had been withdrawn since they had not had a letter of acceptance from our solicitors. In quick succession we sacked our solicitors and employed a more efficient firm who sorted out the hiccough with the GLC. We moved ourselves from Coralline Walk to Roydene Road on a foggy day, using something not much larger than a Ford Transit van. It seemed to take for ever. While replacing the plumbing, I investigated sorting out some heating for the little house. A company called Autocon Engineering was pioneering the selling of microbore central heating systems using rolls of small-bore nylon tubing instead of copper pipes to connect the boiler with the radiators, thus saving money. This appealed to me as it obviated the need for soldered or compression fittings and many lengths of copper pipe. I think I installed the heating for the house for between £300 and £400. I wrote an article about the project for *She* magazine. They liked it a lot, published it entitled 'Curate on Heat' and got their cartoonist Fiddy to do some delightful illustrations. They paid me £25 on acceptance which helped to pay for the odd radiator or two.

For a few years, maybe five, I commuted to and from Thamesmead. I didn't spend any less time at work. Work was all consuming, much to do each day and meetings most evenings.

One night I was in a meeting of the Thamesmead Community Association in the Stage 2 Clubroom at Limestone Walk. Adrian Barnard was there too. At around ten o'clock, the door opened, and Sally Thompson waved to me to get me out of the meeting. 'Annette has been attacked, she's alright, but you need to get back to Roydene Road as soon as you can.' Adrian and I drove as fast as we dared. When we arrived, we were told by policeman not to walk quickly or run as there were police dogs on the loose.

So, we walked up to the house. Annette had gone out to the garden to get the washing in from the machine installed in what had once been an outside lavatory. She saw a shadowy figure in the bushes across the lawn and challenged it. The man chased her into the house. She was about to run out of the front door to escape from him when she thought of Stephen sleeping soundly upstairs. The man grabbed her and beat her up, breaking her nose. She shouted and screamed, and the man ran off into the dark on Plumstead Common, part of which the house faced. Annette was taken to hospital. She miscarried as a result of this beating and shock.

The perpetrator was never found. A few days after the incident a senior policeman called at the house wanting to ask some questions. He wanted to know if there was anyone I knew locally or at work who would have done such a thing. There was not, I said. Annette was still in shock, but she remembers that she felt the police did not believe a single word she told them.

'This is all very difficult. Nothing like this has happened on my patch in the last eighteen months,' said the policeman, I think an inspector. I managed not to rise and murder him. The attacker was still at large, and I felt as if we were being asked to feel sorry for ruining the policeman's faultless record. I felt more anger towards the police than I did towards the perpetrator. I suspected he was probably mad or at least mentally deranged. He didn't attempt to steal anything. This took place before police were trained how to treat victims but we both felt outraged by the police's approach.

A day or two after the event, the local parish priest from St Mark and St Margaret's Church called on us and said we should get into his car and he would take us to get a dog. He drove us somewhere into Kent and we returned to our little house with an exceptionally large dog. We called him Dougal. I think he was a cross between a black Labrador and a great Dane. Imagine a Labrador on stilts. I once crammed him onto a weighing machine at a railway station and found that he weighed all of four and a half stone. Unlike very many Labradors, he had not an ounce of fat on him, he was all muscle and bone. One Boxing Day we took him down to see the English Channel. He rushed into the sea and rushed out again. The next morning, we knew he was ill as he wouldn't even look at his breakfast. We took him to a vet who said, 'Pop him up on the table, please,' and that's when I found out just how heavy he was. The vet examined him, looked at his throat and said he had tonsillitis, sold us some expensive drug to give Dougal and in no time at all he was as right as rain. He was the scariest looking and yet the gentlest dog I have ever met. He was the first of three Labrador-type dogs we had over some thirty years.

Dougal liked nothing better than sitting on everyone's lap, one after the other if, for example, the babysitting circle was meeting at our house. He, like many of his kind, stole food whenever he could but grinned as he did so. 'It's what we do,' he seemed to say. He could run like the wind. He ran off one day while I was walking him on Plumstead Common. I found him later, about a mile away walking along Plumstead High Street. I knew where he had been. His paws were covered in sawdust. He had been visiting butchers' shops. Sometimes he would vanish at night up to the nearest pub, The Old Mill, where he would tell stories about his owners feeding him just once a week and, yes, a packet of crisps would be most acceptable. Twice he arrived back at home by car, once in a taxi he had jumped into, saying 'drive me home,' and jingling his address disc on his collar. On another occasion a pub-goer said, 'He jumped in our car and asked to be taken home.'

Dougal was a great guard dog. Visitors, postmen, meter readers would ask if he was safe and we would reply, 'He hasn't eaten anyone the last day or two.' He would stand looking out of the front windows, his front paws on the low windowsill. One morning, after Annette had gone to college, I was in the kitchen clearing up after breakfast. Looking up the garden which sloped up to a retaining wall, I saw a teenager put his leg over our wall. I quietly opened the back door. There was a streak of black as Dougal raced up to the wall, and the teenager moved faster than he had ever done in his life. Dougal would have made him welcome, but the youth didn't know that. There were no burglaries in our terrace while Dougal was with us. Once we left Roydene Road, we were told that there were twenty burglaries in three months.

One of the possibilities I explored was that of setting up a trust for the development whose purpose would be to find ways to encourage Thamesmead people to have their own ideas, dream their own dreams, and then use the trust to bring these ideas and dreams to birth. A subtext could have been a move away from the dependency culture in which the residents had most decisions removed from them and became consumers of the development rather than architects and planners of their own lives there.

For inspiration and exploration, I visited the North Kensington area of London where land under elevated roads was being developed for community purposes. I went to talk to the Dartington Trust in Devon, about as much of a contrast with North Kensington and Thamesmead as anyone could imagine but the same commitment to creativity and development that I imagined for a possible trust.

Gradually the trust idea took shape. Ideally it would not involve large chunks of money. It would be a limited liability company with charitable objects. I had already discovered the advantages of small, staff-light organisations which had almost no budget and could move without the dead hand of 'point of order, Madam Chairman' delays. Anyone who has had to penetrate the dark corridors and mysterious procedures of housing departments will understand.

I was advised to go and talk to a splendid firm of lawyers, McKenna and Company, at the Trafalgar Square end of Whitehall. There I was mightily encouraged to continue sketching out the aims and objectives which they could translate into a legal framework for a company, limited by guarantee with charitable objects. They did all the legal work and were kind enough not to charge us for it.

Meanwhile the new Bishop of Woolwich David Sheppard took a

great interest in how we were doing. He went with Jim Thompson to see the National Westminster Bank in the City where possible administrative help was discussed. NatWest Enterprises was, I think, formed to give approved organisations help from experienced bank managers who might be moved sideways into groups like ours where they would continue to acquire seniority and commensurate pay and allowances while allowing junior managers with ability to be fast-tracked through the banking ranks. At least, that's how I understood it to work. As a result of Jim describing what was being attempted and achieved at Thamesmead, we were granted the help of Eddie Simmonds from the other side of the Thames to be our administrator. Jim already had a marvellous secretary from the Abbey Wood Estate, Jean Parker, working in the office at the Church of the Cross.

The secondment of Eddie Simmonds was truly timely. Once the trust was set up, we needed a first project to demonstrate what the trust was about and might be able to achieve.

The main road from Abbey Wood Station northward towards the eventual town centre, Harrow Manor Way, was built in elevated form to cross over the sewer bank which housed the enormous sewerage pipes from the southeast of London to Cross Ness sewage treatment works.

Between the vertical supports for the elevated road, there were enormous half-walled areas which, ignored, would quickly become litter-infested waste dumps where all manner of rubbish could be tipped or unsavoury activities could develop. Why not enclose them and turn them into useful community areas?

We applied to the GLC for the lease of these spaces. This was readily granted as the GLC didn't want them to become community eyesores any more than we did. The architects were hugely helpful and a scheme to enclose the arches was designed.

The plan was to complete the enclosure of the first three arches. We thought that the one in the middle could be tastefully enclosed and used for all manner of artistic endeavours, while the arches either side might be used as an indoor kick-about area at one end and a community furniture store at the lower end. The only condition imposed by the GLC was the necessary one of access to the underneath of the road structure for maintenance or repair.

We then gave some thought to the question of who would do the building and other work to transform the arches into usable spaces. By some glorious coincidence, the government was promoting and paying for job creation schemes. The idea was that young and otherwise unemployable people could be put to work on a community scheme after which they would be ready for the world of work, and, better yet, employable. We applied to run such a scheme and were given the go ahead. This is where Eddie Simmonds became involved. He knew everything there was to know about financial records, bookkeeping, and accounting procedures, and enough about dealing with government departments, huge areas of massive ignorance in my case. I could not have considered applying for a job creation scheme without Eddie's administrative skills.

We took on ten unemployed and unemployable young men, and two out-of-work skilled foremen to act as supervisors and trainers. We worked with Thamesmead architects and Church of the Cross member and architect Peter Goodwin, to produce a design for enclosing the arches, basic security fencing for the first and third arches, and a fully enclosed area for the middle arch.

The plans called for building, plumbing, electrical, glazing, and painting and decorating skills. The design for the middle of the three arches called for a large quantity of toughened glass, scaffold poles, a Portakabin. I set about writing letters begging for such materials for the project. Now Trust Thamesmead was in being, had its own headed notepaper, and I was the company secretary. What could possibly go wrong?

We were much blessed in the response. The main contractors, Cubitts, had a great quantity of scaffold poles they didn't want as they were pulling off the site. Pilkingtons Glass at St Helens, Lancashire, had a large quantity of toughened plate glass ready to be used or thrown back into the furnace after a Middle East deal had fallen through just before shipment. If we could cut it, we could have it.

We didn't let on to the community what the eventual activities might be under these arches. Instead we let them know through *Insight* what areas we were enclosing and asked them to scratch their heads and decide what they would like to do with the spaces. They should write to the trust with their proposals, and the most imaginative schemes and community groups would be offered the spaces for them to use as they saw fit. The trust wasn't interested in the management of the arches; this would be the community's responsibility. Besides, we didn't have the staff or the energy to manage the spaces. That was up to them.

When the replies came in, there was no shortage of ideas. The Thamesmead Football Club, thriving under the leadership of Jim Adie, asked for the tallest space as a floodlit kick-about all-weather area for the club. Thamesmead Arts Club asked for the glazed central space that they could use around the year for art, drama, pottery, and dance. The third space was indeed used as a used furniture store as the headroom was too low for other than storage purposes.

This project was a test of the trust's principles, to encourage Thamesmead people to dream their own dreams and then use the mechanism of the trust to help bring those dreams to birth. It seemed to me that this was another case of everybody winning. The arches would have filled up with litter and rubbish. With our scheme, Thamesmead people gained three very large spaces which were secure. They were able to do what they wanted; learn how to administer the spaces they had chosen. Unemployable teenagers were taught skills which then helped them into employment. Everybody won. I call this the mad mathematics of the gospel. It works with jumble sales. People get rid of stuff they don't want or need. Others buy what they think they want or need. The remainder is carted off for recycling or other purposes, people have a chance to meet socially, and money is raised for good causes. Fantastic. I suppose I learned enough about jumble sales at Yeovil to be able to write a piece for the *Guardian* which they published under the heading 'The Jumblies.' Another winner from the process. And they paid me £8 for the article.

When we left Thamesmead, the trust continued under the leadership of Maureen Chambers. Before the Greater London Council was dissolved by Margaret Thatcher, the trust was given a grant of over a million pounds which, I believe, was used to build Thamesmead's first swimming pool. Eventually the trust was absorbed into the Peabody organisation in 2014 and Peabody became the principal developer of Thamesmead, responsible for housing and community facilities. 'Trust Thamesmead – Together we can,' a good slogan if ever there was. I wish I'd thought of it!

Another project which occurred to me as a mad idea was the possibility of community television on the Thamesmead cable system. There was a cable system serving some housing in the Woolwich area. It was called Greenwich Cablevision and I had some involvement with it. It was Greenwich Cablevision who came and filmed the opening of the Church of the Cross and whose equipment was stolen later that same night. I once made a documentary about an Abbey Wood estate playgroup. When I got the videotapes back to the offices of Greenwich Cablevision, I was shown just once how to perform a jump edit from the one video tape machine to another. It was very primitive and not a little scary. Other than that, I contributed some short religious bits to camera on Saturday mornings. The studio was in a ground floor garage at the base of a tall block of flats in Plumstead, premises which sometimes flooded during or after heavy rain. My piece was always broadcast live after the film programme, whose presenter peppered his scripts with several 'and finally . . .' phrases before continuing for a further few minutes.

Thamesmead was served for radio and television programmes by a cable which had outlets in each home. When we first published *Insight*, we would write readers' letters over daft pseudonyms like I D Clare, to encourage readers to write in on matters that excited or bothered them. The people of Thamesmead in those early years were from parts of London, especially the East End, where you could have your ear bent on any topic under the sun and then some. Letter writing was more of a challenge. So, thinking about this and the availability of the cable, I wondered about community television. Over the years I had opened a file about it and filled it with all sorts of information around the possibility of it happening at Thamesmead.

One day, thinking that I should make some progress with community television on the Thamesmead cable if only to get on with it or throw away the research file, I made an appointment to see someone at Rediffusion's regional office in Basildon. I asked about community television on the Thamesmead cable and was told very firmly that it was an idea that would not fly. Why, I asked. 'The government won't approve it, and even if they did, you couldn't afford it. But,' said the man, 'did you know the Home Office is looking for applications from people wanting to try community radio?' I said I hadn't heard about that. 'You'll have to hurry; I think the closing date for applications is tomorrow.'

I left in a hurry and drove like a maniac back to Thamesmead, where I sat down in the office at the Church of the Cross and typed a letter to the Home Office on, I think, just one side of a sheet of A4 paper. I also rang them up to ask them to hold the deadline open until my letter got there. They said they would.

There wasn't time to talk to anyone about this, and I wasn't entirely convinced that the idea would work, but if I didn't apply, I wouldn't find out. I posted the letter and forgot all about it in the unending list of other things that needed doing.

Six months later, to my horror, surprise, and joy, I received a letter from the Home Office who, in those days oversaw prisons, the police, immigration, and broadcasting. They said I was to have a licence to originate community broadcasting on the Thamesmead cable. Oh, and the licence would cost £1,265. We named the project Insound.

Back I went to the lawyers McKenna and Company of Whitehall to ask if they could help set up a company to hold the licence and enable broadcasting to happen at Thamesmead. They found a company, Premierworth, lying redundant on a shelf and said I could have that, and they would revise the aims and objectives of the company to allow it to broadcast. We were almost in business, and bless them, as with setting up Trust Thamesmead, they made no charge for their services.

It was agreed that Insound could use a small room in the new shared church, St Paul's, in what was expected to one day become Thamesmead's town centre. I may have known a little about radio, but the world of real broadcasting was almost a closed book to me. I took advice from wherever I could, typed more begging letters, and my former employers, now Associated Electrical Industries of Woolwich sent me, I think, £25, enough to buy a kettle. I found a retailer in West London who let me have some Sony equipment at trade prices.

In a very cheeky move, I went to see the managing director of Capital Radio at Euston Tower, John Whitney, a member of the Society of Friends and he generously gave me £500 towards the project. I had also asked one of his presenters, Adrian Love, if he would kindly come and open the radio station. He agreed. Adrian was interviewed for a local paper feature on this new kind of radio station. 'The problem we have at Capital is that we're trying to be all things to all men,' he said. 'We have the largest local radio station in the world with a potential audience of 12,500,000. You're trying to talk to people in Enfield and Ealing and you can't. In the case of Insound, it's great because you are talking to people who live in Thamesmead. It's a very good thing to have community radio. To be local in London is difficult because we live in a series of villages.' Adrian should have written the licence application.

I found a supplier of cork tiles in Bermondsey and set out to deaden the acoustic of our little studio. A few days after I had covered the walls with the cork tiles, the church had a visit from a fire safety officer who looked with interest at the tiles and asked me if the heating system had been on when I was working there. I said I thought it had been. Somewhat shocked, he told me I was incredibly lucky that I was alive and that the building was still standing. The adhesive for the tiles was petroleum based and the fumes would have left the room and gone looking for a source of ignition, which could have been provided by the central heating gas boiler.

I gathered from this that yes, I was lucky, and that perhaps God was in favour of the project. I found some volunteers to help with the radio station. Member of Parliament James Wellbeloved said he would come to the opening on a Saturday morning. The day before the opening I got a call from Rediffusion's central office in Haymarket, London, asking if I had taken out insurance for cover against libel, infringement of copyright, and other risks I hadn't imagined and probably couldn't spell. I had to admit that it hadn't crossed my mind. 'Well, you can't start broadcasting tomorrow morning unless you can present a cover note for such insurance at this office by close of business this afternoon.'

Suddenly the time that I had put aside to get the opening programme ready for broadcast was all but eaten up in a marathon time on the phone looking for a company who could sell us the appropriate insurance. I found someone, collected a cover note and fought the rush hour traffic streaming out of London to get it into the hands of some responsible person at Rediffusion before they closed for the weekend. I didn't get the go-ahead from them until about 9 p.m. I worked through until about three o'clock in the morning of the Saturday. At 9 a.m., I played in Aaron Copland's *Fanfare for the Common Man*, and Adrian Love opened the first-ever programme from Insound. I think we had one jingle, 'Never a Dull Moment.' Which I guess could be a way to describe our time at Thamesmead, time which I would not have missed for the world, for with God everything was, and is, possible.

The radio station worked, primary school children interviewed local politicians about their work, people talked and talked and talked about everything under the sun. I think we helped to prove the case for community broadcasting. When it celebrated its fifth birthday in January 1983, it was broadcasting for up to twenty-one hours a week on a budget of £8,000 a year, made up of £5,000 from the GLC and the balance from a government youth opportunities programme. Eventually Insound grew into a real radio station with its own VHF frequency serving maybe a quarter of London. While writing this book I learned that plans were being developed for a new radio station for Thamesmead called RTM.FM, programmes being broadcast online. I suspect some of those involved with Insound went on to work in real local radio.

One of the unexpected side effects of setting up Insound was a sudden approach from the Thamesmead Baptist Church who must have thought, 'My God, Insound can get into every home at Thamesmead on a regular basis, perhaps we should be heard, even if it means talking to those people who don't believe the Bible.'

I remember to this day a team meeting during which Jim Thompson looked straight at me and said, 'Patrick, we're going to have to limit you to just one idea a year.' My face must have either gone white as a sheet or fallen a mile or maybe both because, bless him, he went on to add, 'not because they are not good ideas, but because of the consequences.' He was right of course. He generally was. The more I think back to that time, I realise that to have someone on the team who is engaged in a ministry of mad ideas is no bed of roses for colleagues because of the consequences. And because of the stress which may grip not just the originator of the idea, though that undoubtedly happened, but because of the ripples or tidal wave of consequences which affected hours worked and budgets, categories which favour well-behaved, surprise-light activities.

I think it was earlier that I went to see Dr Rodney Turner at Lakeside Health Centre because I was feeling freaked out and exhausted. He put me on some tranquillisers, Valium, Librium, or something, and told me not to work for a fortnight. He asked, 'You feel deeply about things, don't you, Patrick?' I thought about that and agreed that I hoped that was probably true. I think I took myself off the pills very quickly as they made me feel worse, but I did stay off work for the full fortnight. That was certainly not the last time I approached stress or burnout. I had bumped into the endless nature of ministry when I was a curate in Yeovil, and the only thing to do on my day off was to drive off somewhere where I could not be reached, either to see Martha and James for the day at Ashill or to hitch up the trailer and boat and drive down to the coast and set off with Martin Francis into the wide blue or more likely grey yonder. I remember a meeting at the home of Bishop David Sheppard. Somehow the conversation got round to days off. The bishop showed us a wooden soundproof box he had made to fit over his telephone on his day off. Some of the priests were clearly shocked that a bishop should so cut himself off for just one day a week. I wished I had thought of the idea.

The matter of pastoral care of the clergy and the recurring cases of priests becoming stressed is an elephant you might think has only just arrived in the room. I note that work is being done in General Synod to look at workload and breakdown among clergy, and I think I read the other day that consideration was being given to whether or not clergy might have two days off a week.

There used to be a bank with a slogan, 'the bank that likes to say yes.' The notion that yes is the only acceptable answer to any demands made on a priest is the beginning of madness. I write as a fool, I am not good at saying no. A few months ago, my bedside phone woke me shortly before two o'clock on a Saturday morning. It was a carer who was looking after a parishioner's elderly mother while her daughter took a weekend away in the west country. She had fallen asleep watching television and had woken up to find a massive flood in her kitchen. A joint on the mains water inlet pipe had failed. Could I come round and help? I got dressed and found my sea-boots, a couple of adjustable spanners and a pipe wrench and drove the mile or so to the house. I have never seen water spray into a kitchen under such pressure. I managed to get far enough into the cupboard under the sink to start to close the heavy-duty plastic stopcock and the flood abated. Just then the fire brigade arrived and finished the job. We then swept all the water out of the kitchen and an adjoining room, and I finally got home at around 3 a.m.

'For God's sake, pace yourself, Patrick,' said my mother one day. At the time I thought the remark a bit rich coming from someone who never seemed to stop for a moment, a whirlwind writer if ever there was one. But she was right, and I probably have left it too late now to change the habit of a half a century or more. Nonetheless, it matters that we get a grip on what is a reasonable expectation or request and what is plain silly. I remember years and years ago thinking that one of the challenges to the church and to believers is that if all the world must have the gospel preached to it, then the job is infinite. There is always more to do, more people to see, things to remember.

When I think back to the adventure and challenge of Thamesmead, people running like crazy just to stand still, I am not surprised that after nine years it was time to move on. When a kindly Eric James asked me some years after Thamesmead whether I would consider an inner-city post, I thought it best not to say yes. My anxiety would be the temptation of trying to do another Thamesmead in a probably completely inappropriate setting.

Years after Thamesmead I met a delightful worker for one of the great Anglican missionary societies. She told me she had been given some helpful advice during her training. She was told that she should divide each day into three parts and never work for more than two out of the three. It sounded simple and made sense to me, who even then was trying to do three jobs at a time. Jesus in his short ministry took time away from the madness to be alone, to pray, to sit and think or sleep. And I sometimes caught myself wondering what Jesus would have done if his early ministry, if not his entire ministry, had been worked out in Thamesmead. Surely it's not blasphemous to wonder?

As the Church of England continues to shrink, it is as if no-one much has noticed the crisis of staffing the parishes, with priests being put in charge of up to twelve parishes, who once upon a time each had a vicar, rector, or curate. It makes no sense for the church authorities to claim that no-one living in England is beyond the scope and pastoral care of the clergy while so many posts are vacant and so many parishes are lumped together, the responsibility of a single priest. Looking at

The Church Times a few weeks back I was dismayed to see how many posts were being advertised for house-for-duty priests. These are parish jobs where the usually-retired priest is given accommodation presumably with the council tax being paid by the parish or diocese. In return he or she does all he or she can in the way of taking services, pastoral visiting, whatever may need to be done.

A letter to *The Times* about burnt-out clergy in June 2019 brought a reply that painted an accurate picture of the Church of England, with clergy 'expected to oversee and care for churches, often with little assistance. Small wonder that some vacant posts have little likelihood of gaining a permanent incumbent. Congregations are desperate to hang onto 'their church,' often with no thought for the well-being of 'their vicar.' A job advert that begins 'The nine churches of . . .' would make even the most dedicated soul take flight.

In a recent set of statistics, there were over 7,000 stipendiary priests in England and over 7,000 'retired' clergy. The notion of retirement needs a book to itself if only to include all the stories and jokes.

A while back I received an invitation to a meeting for retired clergy to be addressed by a former bishop of the diocese on the subject 'the theology of retirement'. Since I didn't think there could be any such theology in the same way there could be no such retirement, I signed up for the session, anxious to explore whatever the bishop might say on the matter. Significantly, I thought, the bishop wasn't there as he had found he had double-booked himself. Game, set, and match, maybe.

Back at Thamesmead one of the more enjoyable activities at the Church of the Cross was the pantomime. A member of the congregation, a Congregationalist, Margaret Kennard worked in the week for Christian Aid. She wrote some of the pantomime scripts for the church. Jim Thompson also wrote and produced the shows. I particularly remember helping with Alice in Wonderland. Typecast perhaps, I played the Mad Hatter; Martin Booth played the Caterpillar. Our son Stephen played one of the playing cards. His performance and experience so early in his life may have been the foundation for his completing a degree course in performing arts. These shows were great fun and generally well-attended.

Before we left Thamesmead in 1978, we moved from our little house in Plumstead back to Thamesmead to 18 St Helen's Road. The garden was far too small for our lovely dog Dougal, so we gave him away to someone with a larger garden and more time to take him for walks. Not long before we left, we went to the Boat Show at Earl's Court. There we saw a brilliant build-it-yourself Mirror sailing dinghy, designed by Ian Proctor and promoted by *The Daily Mirror*. It was just 10'6" long. We bought a kit.

Weeks later an enormous parcel was delivered. The house had a garage, and the first requirement was to check that all the parts were present and correct. I looked at this growing heap of carefully pre-cut and drilled bits of marine plywood. The thought that it might one day become a sailing dinghy seemed ridiculous.

The Mirror dinghy gradually began to take shape. It was a brilliant design and once all the parts had been identified, it was not as difficult to build as I had thought it might be. The main parts of the hull were held together with copper wire laced through the holes. When the hull was formed all the seams were covered with layers of fibreglass tape soaked in resin. I think the finished hull was lowered out of our first-floor window to the pavement below for finishing in the garage. It would have never fitted down our narrow staircase.

We called the dinghy Magic Penny after a song written by Malvina Reynolds which I used to get children to sing in school assemblies. The theme of the song is that when you give love away there is always more available to be given. 'Love is something if you give it away, you end up having more.'

We launched the boat on South Mere, Thamesmead's first lake. To this day I can't quite believe it floated without a sign of a leak.

CHAPTER 11

A Runcible idea

How to find another post? I think I wrote to someone in the Diocese of St Albans to ask if there were any jobs going there which might work for us. Meanwhile I had a letter from Bishop David Sheppard's successor as Bishop of Woolwich, Michael Marshall. He instructed that I accept no job outside the Diocese of Southwark for a period of thirty days as the diocese was working on a communications post which would be a perfect fit for me. I am so glad I didn't wait as I think the thirty days probably lengthened to a few years. I might still be waiting.

It seems that Jim Thompson had been to a cell meeting with some of his friends, amongst whom was Robert Runcie, around September in 1977. It is likely that while travelling in the bishop's comfortable Ford Ghia that the possibility of a communications officer in Robert's Diocese of St Albans came up. It may be that Jim thought it was something I might be able to do. This is largely conjecture loosely based on odd letters still in what passes for my filing system. On Jim's suggestion, I wrote to Bishop Runcie in October saying I was looking for a move and for some post that would build on my work at Thamesmead. I enclosed a CV and thought that the next piece of work might last eight to ten years as 'I don't think flitting around from job to job is useful to anyone.'

Eric James, the Canon Missioner for the Diocese of St Albans, drafted a job description for the post of Information Officer which I received in February 1978. I noted down some reactions to the document including the question, 'What does "half time" mean to the parishes?' I thought that Communications Officer might be a better job title and that he or she should not be a magician who would do laity or clergy communications for them. Whoever was appointed would edit *See Round*, the diocesan monthly with about 40,000 readers. *See Round* was thought to take some three to four days a month to do. The work would include liaising with local press and media outlets with local radio coming to the diocese. There would be close contact with Church Information Office at Church House in London. Looking back at the draft job specification, I am reminded of the discussions around the choosing of a rector for Thamesmead. Too late did I discover that what was being proposed was beyond impossible and that nobody would be satisfied. There was no mention of any secretarial assistance, and any expenses apart from mileage at the diocesan rate were 'a matter of conjecture.'

I was asked to apply for the post of priest in charge of two village parishes: Offley and Lilley between Hitchin, Hertfordshire, and Luton in Bedfordshire. This was to be one half of the job; the other half was to be the diocesan Communications Officer for St Albans Diocese.

We travelled to Hertfordshire, met the Rural Dean, Canon Peter Pavey, looked round Offley and Lilley. Offley Vicarage was quite grand, in Kings Walden Road, almost opposite the churchyard and very near to a pub, the Red Lion. The house had been built in 1938 as had I, with five bedrooms, study with separate entrance for parishioners, cloakroom, sitting room, dining room, kitchen, butler's pantry, maid's sewing room. It had a system of bells which whenever we playfully rang them, produced no maid or butler. There was a garage and an acre of garden. A villager, Frank Carter, used a small part of the garden as an allotment and often we would find some of his vegetables waiting on our doorstep.

We were both duly interviewed by a joint meeting of the two parochial church councils. Annette was asked what she was going to do. She said she would complete her teacher training course, look after me and Stephen, and then see what else was possible. I think they were looking for a vicar's wife who would take on all manner of parish jobs.

14 East Street, Lilley, formerly The Red Lion

For the life of me I have no recollection of any questions they asked me. Probably just as well.

Whatever we made from the sale of the house in St Helen's Road at Thamesmead was quickly swallowed up by the cost of a new Volkswagen Polo, and curtains and carpets for the vicarage at Great Offley. Because we had so much grass to cut and no sign of a gardener, we bought a petrol motor mower for £250 which we wore out in the five years we were there.

Stephen enrolled in the village school and the head teacher Mr Foley quickly determined that he was a good year behind the top juniors' class into which he moved. To their great credit, in a year Stephen had caught up with his contemporaries. I was de facto chairman of two sets of school governors for the schools at Offley and Lilley, roles for which I was completely unprepared and probably unqualified. School governors now probably look back to the late seventies and eighties with nostalgia for less bureaucracy or interference by official bodies from the church or county authorities.

The Forbeses of Lilley, including Laddie the Labrador

Becoming a sort of parish priest again was a considerable culture shock. If the parish scene was challenging, holding down half a job for the diocese proved not to be a bed of roses either.

I discovered that some three years earlier Bishop Runcie had asked the Diocesan Synod to appoint a communications officer as part of a three-year plan for the diocese. The request was decisively laughed out of court. However, such appointments were beginning to be made around the country as bits of the church began to think that communications within dioceses might just matter and that there was a growing number of media outlets which needed attention.

Once I had been appointed as priest in charge of Offley and Lilley, the bishop then told the diocese he was sure they would not mind if I helped him with some of his communications work, adding that a contribution to the expenses of such work might not come amiss. Diocesan Synod agreed. I think it was not until we were four or five years into the diocese that my expenses were finally put on a proper basis.

The diocese probably grumbled to itself. Yes, maybe some office space might be found for me at the diocesan office in St Albans. In the meantime, perhaps I could have a corner of a desk in Robert Runcie's office in his home, Abbey Gate House.

I was there one day when in strode the Dean's Administrator, a retired Admiral. Robert Runcie introduced me to him and said I would be editing *See Round*. The Admiral harrumphed and said something like, 'Huh, *See Round*, can't think why anyone would bother with that.' The diocesan office repeatedly failed to find me somewhere to sit or perch as Canon Eric James had suggested. 'It's all very difficult,' I was told time after time when I rang to enquire. After some six months of this nonsense, I finally cracked. I drove from Offley into Hitchin, bought a roof rack for the Volkswagen and bought a second-hand desk from a dealer in Walsworth Road. I tied it onto the roof rack and drove to St Albans where I parked in the diocesan office car park. I unloaded the desk, opened a ground floor window, and manhandled the desk through it. I slapped the invoice down and asked someone to pay me back and find a space where I could sit and work.

I suspect that didn't go down too well, and I was first given a tiny space in the post room, a singularly noisy and uncomfortable place to be. It was, however, a start. Eventually I was found a little office squeezed between similarly small offices for the social responsibility officer, David Skidmore, and the diocesan adult education officer, Jean Stilwell, in a temporary building called the Garden Offices down a path from the diocesan office and opposite the house of the Canon Missioner, Eric James, who had also migrated from Southwark Diocese.

Someone had to decide how on earth communications would fit into the diocese's committee structure. Eric James had suggested in his draft of the work of the Information Officer that that person should attend and might be made a member of the Board of Mission and Unity. This committee was chaired a year at a time by the diocesan and suffragan bishops of Bedford and Hertford. The meetings were held in the diocesan office at monthly or two-monthly intervals and lasted perhaps two hours. Somewhere, way down the agenda, would be the Communications Officer's report for which I would be responsible. At one such meeting I remember feeling convinced that no-one could give a toss, so when the bishop asked me to give my report, I stood up and reported, 'Bishop, things happen.' I sat down. I am not even sure if anyone asked a question. Which meant, of course, we could all go home a bit earlier.

St Mary Magdalene Church, Great Offley was a mess. Worse, it was a cold and damp mess needing, some said, around £90,000 to be raised and spent on it, just to repair what was obviously wrong. On the north side of the church there was an electric boiler which heated water that then circulated around the radiators. This system leaked and I religiously topped it up each week. The Roman Catholics in the villages had been asked to think of the church in Hitchin as their spiritual home, rather as we had been asked if we would relate to the main parish church in Hitchin. They were as unimpressed as we were. So, a delightful Roman Catholic priest, Father Christopher, would come out from Hitchin on a Wednesday each month to celebrate a mass for Roman Catholic villagers. More than once I asked him if he would like to have what had once been a Roman Catholic church back. He would laugh and say, 'Not on your life, Patrick. I'm not that daft.'

I don't doubt that once upon a time, perhaps in the fourteenth century, it might have been a welcoming medieval church. People would have stood for the services, with the weakest going to the wall to stand or to sit on a ledge. Now it was cursed with a Georgian chancel added by the local family and far too much statuary by Joseph Nollekens, a sculptor praised for his busts. On bad days I might catch myself wondering whether Offley Church might catch fire one day. Then I would realise that of course it would not, it was far too damp. A fine example of the classic medieval self-extinguishing church. Great Offley sits on a hill in generally flat Hertfordshire. I used to imagine winds being born in the Ural Mountains of Russia, pushing westward across the Baltic, picking up moisture from the North Sea, and dumping snow and rain and cold on Great Offley. It was certainly the coldest, dampest church I have ever encountered.

St Peter's Church, Lilley was hugely different. In Victorian times the rector of Lilley, a Mr Haviland, thought to be one of the wealthiest priests in the land, on finding that the medieval church was unsafe, had it taken down and replaced with a sweet little church. It is believed he paid for this work, and for the building of a twelve-bedroom rectory and the village school. The rectory was later demolished and some very pleasant and, I imagine, expensive houses were built on the site, now called Greenacres.

When we arrived in Great Offley, we found that St Peter's had just three bells. People who wanted to be married there would ask about bells being rung for their wedding. I felt obliged to warn them off as the bells were not in good condition, one was cracked, and another was out of tune. To their enormous credit, local people resolved to remedy the situation, and found the money to have the bells repaired and retuned, and for a further three bells to be bought, making a ring of six bells. While the bells were being repaired the villagers rebuilt and renovated the oak bell frame under supervision from a diocesan expert. Three discordant bells will not enhance any wedding ceremony, while a ring of six bells is something wonderful to hear, whether at a wedding or the weekly Sunday service. I was able to recommend having the bells rung for weddings. Being a sweet little village, many people who lived in Luton wondered and sometimes asked if they could be married in Lilley. And, although the rules of weddings have been relaxed somewhat, unless there is a family connection with the village, by and large the answer must be no. An archbishop's licence may be obtained, costing at the time of writing something north of four hundred pounds. But there must be cogent reasons why such a licence might be sought or granted.

One of the first tasks I was expected to take on was to produce the Offley and Lilley church monthly magazine. This was, I think, the least attractive publication I have ever seen, only rivalled by the infant *Mesmedaath* at Thamesmead, mercifully strangled by its fourth edition. It was six pages of foolscap paper, squeezed ink duplicated on a dreadful Gestetner duplicator which seemed to come with Offley Vicarage. This Gestetner would accept a stencil, lovingly prepared and smelling of many pink-coloured corrections. I would load up the machine, with, say, a hundred sheets, and turn the handle, then spend perhaps twenty minutes trying to find the twenty copies the machine had deigned to produce. The publication was a nightmare. It was not delivered house to house, nor was it free.

As it seemed I was expected to put the whole thing together, print it, staple it, and sell it, something had to give before I did. I started to produce something called *Village Voice* which in the beginning was A4, folded, printed with graphics, illustrations, headlines, none of which had featured in its predecessor. It was distributed free each month to everyone in Offley, Lilley, Cockernhoe, and, I think, Tea Green. In no time at all, someone in Lilley volunteered to take on the role of editor, others took on advertising sales, admin, and distribution.

When last I saw it, it was doing well, had generated enough profit to inaugurate a fund to help village projects and community endeavours.

St Peter's, Lilley

The advertisements take up about 50 per cent of the space, but there is plenty of room for village news, comments, and stories.

I enjoyed my relationship with the two schools. I took regular riotous assemblies and however tired or drained I may have felt as I entered the school, I always left on a high, my spirits lifted by the children. Primary school children are so interested, engaged and ready to contribute. I sometimes drove the schools' minibus on excursions to nature reserves or other places. On one such journey back to Lilley from Stevenage, as I drove carefully into the village, a builder's lorry came crashing towards me. I drove as far as I could into the left-hand side of the road, scraping the van sides along the hedge. None of the children was hurt. I jumped out of the minibus with my camera and before I had taken any pictures of the lorry's skid marks, and the relative positions of the two vehicles, the lorry driver pointed at the camera and asked, 'What's that for?' 'Evidence,' I replied, and useful evidence it proved to be. Our insurance claim together with the pictures was handled and completed without question or argument.

Offley had a population of 900 and Lilley between 300 and 400. Numbers of children in Lilley dropped temporarily and the County Council jumped at the chance of closing the little school. The governors, parents, and the village fought the decision right up to the Minister of Education, insisting that the fall in the number of children was temporary and that to close the school would be a huge error. We failed to get the decision reversed and Lilley children had to be taken up to Offley School.

The next battle was with the diocese over the question of what the school building should become. They favoured selling so that a big house could be built on the site. We fought this and persuaded the authorities that it would be better to sell the property so that it could be converted into flats, adding to the housing mix in the village. I think this was a better outcome.

We had always wanted to have another child, but never quite managed it. Annette miscarried on several occasions. We both went through investigations, but nothing availed. We had not been helped by our doctor in Plumstead who, on being asked for help, said, 'I can't see why you want another one!'

The last occasion on which Annette miscarried was after she had passed the critical three-month stage in the pregnancy in the early summer of 1979. It was a Saturday and she miscarried at home. I rang the surgery in Hitchin and was told to keep the foetus so that the doctor could look at it when he would call on the Monday. I was completely emotionally incapable of taking the Sunday services in Offley and Lilley and fortunately they were taken by another member of the country group of priests. All I wanted to do was to be with Annette and cope with the grief we both felt. Robin Oakley, the rector of Ickleford rang up and kindly offered to bring Communion to the house. I thanked him but said I didn't think we could cope with the Sacrament.

On the Monday, the doctor duly called, looked at the evidence which I had placed in a washing up bowl, and said I was free to dispose of it. Emptying a once and future child down the drain felt appalling. I cried. Sometimes it feels as if people may very well be doing their best, but it doesn't quite feel like it at the time. Only years later did I discover that there is an organisation which ministers to people who miscarry or suffer still births.

Sometime later, getting towards Christmas, we agreed that I should go and be sterilised to prevent any further pregnancies or miscarriages. We went to the Marie Stopes Clinic in London where the snip was done, and I remember walking in a rather careful manner at all the Christmas services. Mercifully, the sterilisation didn't turn me into a counter tenor, though I do wonder sometimes just what sort of singing voice I do have, other than loud.

As I once reported to the Board of Mission and Unity, things went on. Annette finished her teacher training course and looked for a teaching post. In Margaret Thatcher's time they seemed to be few and far between. Unable to find a post, Annette took a job as secretary to the head of St Christopher's School, Letchworth. One of the perks was that we could send Stephen to St Christopher's for just a third of the fees that would otherwise be payable. The school was founded in 1915 around the time of the building of Letchworth Garden City, the world's first such development. It has a reputation as 'not your typical public school.' From sinking without trace at Bowes Lyon School – the only teacher who regretted his move was the athletics teacher – Stephen quickly began to thrive at St Chris. He became involved in drama, performing, directing, and music. He played the drums and the guitar. He began to write his own songs and formed a band, the Great Woolly Lettuce, for which Annette created a fantastic fabric lettuce. He became involved with the Quaker Youth Theatre, travelling to Russia with the group to perform in Moscow. From St Christopher School, Stephen went on to study at Middlesex Polytechnic where he gained a degree in performance arts.

Annette's main subject at teacher training college had been embroidery. We still have some of her embroideries, an amazing one representing foxgloves hangs in our living room. At Offley, she discovered people who were keen to sell artwork, pictures they had painted, objects they had made and so she organised craft mornings at the vicarage. She did some voluntary work at a hospital unit for older people in Luton, encouraging patients to draw and paint.

Annette continued to look for a teaching post and finally was appointed head of the nursery unit at Tithe Farm, Houghton Regis, where she spent eleven years, only leaving when voluntary redundancy was offered. One day I was asked to help a party of three-to-four-year olds on a visit to Standalone Farm in Letchworth. One of the little people grabbed my trouser leg and asked, ''Ere mister, what's that black lumpy thing over there?' I looked where he was pointing and said, 'That's a horse.'

Annette was not just a teacher, but an artist and a dancer. Soon after we arrived in Hertfordshire, she joined the Capriol Society for

Annette, second from right with the Capriol dancers

The dragon meets his match in Aylesbury in 2009!

Early Dance, based in Cambridge and founded in 1979. They meet in a parish church hall in Cambridge on Tuesday evenings during three terms a year and are asked to present dances and workshops in schools and colleges. Once a year they take part in the Stourbridge Fair at the Leper Chapel in Cambridge.

Annette made her costumes for this dancing, covering Medieval, Tudor, and Renaissance periods and styles. When she had a cancerous lump removed in the 1980s, she was recovering at home and suddenly thought, 'I should be dancing in Cambridge.' In no time at all she was off to Capriol. Dancing as an aid to recovery.

I hadn't given up on my habit of learning a little bit more. I signed up for an Open University degree course. Because I had technical qualifications, had done some theology, and had a diploma in sociology, I was granted the maximum credit exemptions. Doing these courses was really challenging. Luckily one of my gifts is being able to write quickly. Once or twice, I had to deliver written assignments to my supervisor at her home in Cambridge as clocks counted down the minutes to the day after the deadline date. I took the Arts Foundation course wherein a difficult challenge was doing nothing but look at an old master's painting of Christ being taken down from the Cross, and then having to write coherently about what I had seen. Another course was on Man-Made Futures, looking at the world in the light of new technology and concerns about the future. This was right up my street. I eventually graduated in 1982, and Ma took great pleasure in addressing letters to me 'The Reverend Patrick Forbes, B. A.' I had finally made it to university, albeit one that worked without residential learning other than summer schools.

Wherever we have been Annette has contributed artistic endeavour to the parishes, liturgical dance at Thamesmead, then art and craft sales at Great Offley. She took some eighteen months to design and work a large white altar frontal for St Peter's Church, Lilley. I remember it took eighteen months as the only available space for her large embroidery frame was in our bedroom.

In Hinxworth there is her needlework picture of St Nicholas in an oak frame on the west wall of the church. Annette and I and others plotted and planned the removal of the Victorian rotting pine fixed pews from the church and their replacement by tailor-made movable pews in American oak manufactured by Irish Contract Seating. There was some early resistance to the change and a letter was sent by the protesters to the diocesan bishop, Christopher Herbert, which I rejoice to say he ignored or lost.

One other despicable break with tradition was that when we arrived in Hinxworth during a vacancy, I found that the altar was placed hard against the east wall of St Nicholas Church. I fear that I moved it, so that I could face the congregation at the Sunday Eucharist. I believe they welcomed this disturbance of the holy table. The roof didn't fall in, but the next rector of Ashwell may have received a letter from the archdeacon stating that the altar must never be moved by so much as a quarter of an inch from its new, grudgingly authorised position.

Removing the old pews and clearing the space at the back of the

Altar frontal embroidered by Annette, St Peter's

church made presenting concerts and other activities much easier. Churchwarden Geoff Burrows designed a beautiful oak screen and door into the vestry to replace the ugly stud partition and door that were in place before. Through the glass above the screen we can now see into the ringing chamber. The organ was also moved into the southwest corner of the nave. The chancel works well for small music groups while the rear of the nave has accommodated between twenty and thirty musicians at a time. The pews can be turned round in just fifteen minutes, something that was impossible before.

As an example of the nonsense involved in rules and regulation concerning alterations to churches, in changing from a wooden floor at the west end of the nave to masonry tiles, the diocese insisted that an ecclesiastical archaeologist be present while the work was done. This was presumably in case we discovered the corpse of a king or the bones of an ancient abbot.

Nothing so exciting was found. We should have thought to enclose in an oak frame the one thing that was found, a sweet wrapper carefully dated to the 1950s. For that ecclesiastical archaeologist who someone said was seen sleeping in his van, we were charged around £2,000, an expensive and clearly valuable wrapper. We should have exhibited it in its own case and told the story of over £2,000 down the drain.

One day in 1979 I went to Robert Runcie's office in St Albans. Just inside the door stood the bishop. 'Ah,' he said, 'Patrick, just the person I wanted to see.' I remember thinking, 'What now?' He said, 'Can you think of anyone in the diocese who would benefit from a month-long intensive radio production course in Cambridge?' I said yes. He said, 'Who?' I said, 'Me.' This has echoes of that question in 1956 about a possible trip on a trawler. Saying yes has got me into all sorts of situations, and I have absolutely no doubt at all that they have been right, however stretching or uncomfortable. I learned many years later that I was the unwitting beneficiary of the generous offer of a place on that course by Chris Rees, who at the time was a religious programmes producer at the BBC working for both Radio 2 and Radio 4. Much was to flow from the bishop's question and my answer.

It seemed to make sense, commercial local radio was coming to the area and the church had to be involved at some level. The Cambridge Radio Course was an initiative by the legendary designer of Neve studio sound mixing equipment, Rupert Neve. He was anxious to train Christians who might already be or in future be involved in broadcasting.

Before I went on the course in August 1979, Bishop Runcie called me into his office one day. He told me in the strictest confidence that he had been asked if he would agree to being the next Archbishop of Canterbury. He had not decided if he would agree. Subsequently I learned that he had serious misgivings about the proposal. Should he agree, he said, he would have to have a press release ready for when the announcement would be made. I was to write it. We arranged a time when I could interview him and then write the press release. I recorded my conversation with him and drafted the potential press release. It ran to six sides of A4, unusually long for a press release but the world would need to know his life story, where he grew up, his service in the army, how he won the Military Cross and then his progress through the Church of England. I kept the draft close to me and took it with me to the Cambridge Radio Course.

The intensive Cambridge Radio Course was an eye opener. The thought of training people like me to be radio producers in just four weeks makes me shiver just to think of it. The course took Mondays to Saturdays, kindly letting priests like me off for the Sunday to return and take services in their parishes, which in my case would be 9.30 in Lilley, 11 a.m. in Offley and often an evening service at the Methodist Chapel or the parish church in Offley. On the course, which was accommodated in 1979 in St Catherine's College, we were encouraged to think deeply about the process of broadcasting, about the listener, the theology of communication. We learned the basics of interviewing, writing for radio, the business of editing – practical and theoretical. Editing was still accomplished using a Chinagraph pencil to mark the recording tape, and an aluminium editing block in which the tape was cut diagonally with a single-sided razor blade. We were given exercises to do. 'Go and make a documentary, Patrick.' My group agreed to making a short programme about the River Cam. That was fun. We needed the sound of someone jumping into the river with which to end the programme. I ended up having to jump into the river at least twice because the first time I did, my fellow student who was operating the Uher tape recorder forgot to take his finger off the pause button and nothing was recorded. I jumped in a second time and we had our sound effect. I was shocked at how cold the river could be in August. Another programme exercise became a spoof exploring the consequences of a proposal to turn King's College Chapel into a local radio station. One or two tourists interviewed about the possibility thought it was a wonderful idea. I remember interviewing Rupert Neve on the alterations that would be needed to be made to King Henry VI's masterpiece to ensure there was a good acoustic.

Another exercise was the writing of a 'Thought for the Day.' By now

I was able to write about the final miscarriage back in Offley. And, perhaps strangely, in writing about it I was able to come to terms with what had happened and to finally see that God was there too in the story. I learned later that the fact that I was awarded a distinction on my course completion certificate was because of that piece of writing. It was, too, confirmation of how so much can be communicated through a really short story.

One Sunday when someone else in the country group of parishes must have taken the Offley and Lilley services for me, we were divided into teams to go and record live church services in churches around Cambridge. The team I was in were given a service of Anglican matins to record. I have mentioned elsewhere that this is one of my least favourite services. At the end of the exercise, I was complimented on 'almost making the service bearable.' Editing always makes things better, I have discovered. Radio programmes, sermons, films, talks, articles, all benefit. I learned later that there is a mechanism in the human brain that samples what it is hearing at around eleven-second intervals in order to judge whether to continue listening. That ought to terrify anyone involved in preaching or public speaking of any kind.

One day during the course, Bishop Runcie's secretary rang to say that the bishop needed to have the draft press release. Would I fax it to her? I said I would not, it was far too sensitive a document to be risked going to the wrong number or being seen by anyone else. I said I would personally deliver it to her that afternoon. I drove to St Albans, feeling just a little bit James Bond-like, and handed over the document. I think the bishop must have approved as I think he only altered one word in the entire document.

Came the day when the official announcement about Robert Runcie's appointment was to be made. I travelled to London, arriving at Church House in good time for the press conference around eleven o'clock. I was met on the steps of Church House by the chief press officer for the Church of England, John Miles. He was clearly upset. 'How could you?' he asked me. I really had no idea what he was talking about. It transpired that one of the local newspapers serving the diocese had broken the story that morning. Given the fact that Her Majesty the Queen and the Prime Minister were involved in the appointment, this was a disaster. I really try not to be angry, but I became as angry as John Miles was, but with him for thinking that I had been involved in this leak. I knew I had not and given the trouble I had taken to keep the matter a closely guarded secret, I hoped I would have been trusted.

Before the press conference, the future Archbishop asked me to see him. He said that I would receive a letter from the Office of the Prime Minister asking me if I could throw any light on this matter. I was to reply saying that the Archbishop-designate Robert Runcie had instructed me to say that I had no information to give him. In a few days, I received the letter from Downing Street and replied as I had been told to do. That was the end of the matter as far as I was concerned. I heard later that a local paper had rung the bishop's house a day or so before the day of the announcement, had put three and seven together, made a lucky hundred out of the calculation, and had hit gold, and made my life a bit more difficult, if only for an hour or two.

In the diocese, a local commercial radio licence was on offer. I was asked to join one of the two rival groups intending to bid for the licence. Over many months we worked away at planning programmes, looking for premises which might convert to being a radio station. In the end the Independent Broadcasting Authority rejected our Luton Bedford Radio bid in favour of that put forward by Chiltern Radio. Their headquarters was a converted school in Chiltern Road, Dunstable. The first time I went there, there was a Portakabin from which the broadcasting was being done.

A group of us in the diocese had got together to prepare for contributing some religious programme content to whoever won the franchise. The group was made up of a Baptist minister from Bedford, Peter Stephenson; Baptist minister John Matthews, married to another Baptist minister, Ruth, who worked at Grove Hill shared church in

Hemel Hempstead; Baptist John Peters from St Albans; and Ray Goodship from Cople near Bedford.

We went to the Churches Television Centre at Bushey, an enterprise funded by the Rank Foundation. Here were state-of-the-art radio and television studios and facilities, technical and training staff who ran courses for the likes of us, for business and professional individuals and enterprises.

I remember being told at CTVC that I would never do anything in television. It was a great pleasure to be able to prove them wrong as I wrote and performed any number of epilogues for Anglia Television, appeared on a number of occasions on television in the London area, not least in a fun event walking on water across St Katharine Dock on inflatable water skis for a Michael Aspel Friday evening programme. I also made a series of short programmes about the work of bishops for Anglia. I have heard that that the epilogues were broadcast after the horror film and before the national anthem was played at the end of transmission. Viewers were thought to fall asleep during the film and wake up during the epilogue and wonder and worry about the plot. One Baptist course member sticks in my mind. Asked to write a 'Thought for the Day' as an exercise, he described the first ever baptism he had conducted. In his story everything went well until a large lady – in his words, the sort of person you could imagine kick-starting a jumbo jet – was to be totally immersed. He could immerse her, but would he be able to bring her upright out of the water? Or would she right herself? His choice of words painted such a vivid picture, I was there and could see it happening. Marvellous.

As a group we volunteered to provide religious broadcasting production for Chiltern Radio. We were welcomed and asked to produce a one-and-a-half-hour live magazine programme at 7 a.m. on Sunday mornings, and five 'Thoughts for the Day' for Mondays to Fridays each week. We also produced and presented Lent courses and documentaries.

Colin Mason was the managing director of Chiltern, Phil Fothergill was the programme controller, and Richard Robinson was the chief engineer, and the station first began broadcasting on 15 October 1981. Our first presenter was the Baptist minister Peter Stephenson. When he moved from Bedford, Methodist Peter Whittaker took on the presenting role. He was followed in 1984 by a church army captain, Barry Amis. I had met Barry in the 1970s when he was at the Church Army Training College in Blackheath. We met again in August 1984 at the Greenbelt Christian Arts Festival. We were joined by Patience Purchas who was a deaconess married to the vicar of Wheathampstead. I guess I sort of evolved as a producer and occasional presenter.

Although the local radio work was probably successful in terms of audience numbers – I believe our programme *Travelling* gained the highest figures on a Sunday at Chiltern – it was very demanding. Often, I would be editing interviews and inserts well into Saturday nights and sometimes Sunday mornings. We encouraged local people to send in scripts for the five 'Thoughts for the Day'. These then had to be recorded, edited, and copied onto a cart, or cartridge, for transmission.

Anyone who has worked in broadcast radio or television will know just how quickly things can fall apart. There's a great story about Radio 4's Sunday programme. Due to one of the live items over-running, the producer realized there wouldn't be time to play a recorded feature about the Pope. Anxious to let the presenter in the studio know about this sudden change in the running order, he pressed what he thought was the correct talkback switch in the control room to speak to the presenter. Alas, he pushed the wrong switch and was heard live saying 'We'll need to kill the Pope.' Fortunately, he was a very resourceful producer and was able to ring the Papal Nuncio in London to explain what had just been said to the Sunday audience.

I once misread the time from the studio clock and crossed to LBC, from whom we took the eight o'clock Independent Radio News a minute early and Chiltern listeners were exposed to a minute of LBC's commercials before the news. On another occasion, I fumbled a commercial cart out of its player and dropped it onto a record that was playing on the record deck beneath. Everyone has a tale to tell of things going wrong. Provided you don't draw people's attention to the glitch, most listeners either don't notice or think to themselves, 'It must be live – accidents happen, would I do any better?'

Every year we would make a point of broadcasting *Travelling* live from the Christian Arts Festival Greenbelt. One year we broadcast a two-hour special live programme, the last hour of which was to be taken by Essex Radio. The ads and news were being put in at Dunstable. We got up early and set everything up. We had a small Honda generator to power the outside broadcast unit. All went well until during the first ad break around 8.15, all the equipment died. Richard Robinson and I dashed outside, he splashed more fuel into the motor generator, I started it up and everything came back on. We heard the assistant in Dunstable say, 'this is the last ad, it's forty-five seconds and the outro is. . . .' Being a consummate professional, Barry had the next record cued up already, and not one listener would have been aware of what had happened. When we came off air, Barry offered me a glass of whisky and we toasted our belief, 'there is a God.' First and maybe the last time I have had a glass of whisky at 9 on a Sunday morning.

Early in 1980 the Bishop of Hertford, Peter Mumford rang me to say he wanted me to go on a mid-service clergy course in July at St George's House, Windsor. St George's House, within the precincts of the castle is, if it is not a contradiction in terms, an Anglican think tank. I readily agreed, thinking it would be good for the parishes to have a month's break from me, it would be fun to write to people from Windsor Castle, and, who knew, it might be a restful month when I could relax and even learn one or two things. There were myths swirling around concerning this course. More than one person told me it was a training place for future bishops. I thought this most unlikely.

CHAPTER 12

Discovering fools, clowns, and more radio

In due course I received a whole heap of paperwork from Windsor. And there was a catch. There always is. I had to research a subject of my choice and, before the course even started, submit ten to twelve thousand words to St George's House. This, with the projects of all the other students, some twenty-five of them, would form some of the material for the course itself. I filled in the form, slapped down the first thing I thought of for the subject of my research, 'The Church and Communications', and sent it off and forgot all about it.

Until, that is, Annette and I were summoned to spend a pre-course day at St George's House, meeting the staff and my tutor and the other course members. I met my tutor, a tall Methodist, Dr John Long, in his book-lined study. He asked me how the project was going. I said it wasn't, too much else was happening. Bless him, he didn't panic but he asked what I had originally selected as my topic. I said, 'the church and communications' but I added that I didn't think the church was interested in communications anymore. There was a silence which endured. 'How about music?' he asked. I said I played the eleven- or twelve-string guitar but didn't read music so that probably wouldn't work. A longer silence followed, and deepened, into which I suddenly heard myself say, 'I know, I've always wanted to explore the relationship between clowns, fools, and the gospel.' I was as surprised as he was, as I had never consciously thought any such thing in my life. It was a pure gift. He may have thought so too, as much relieved, he exclaimed 'No-one's ever done that before, tell me how I can help.' I think by then there were only seven or eight weeks before the course began, so I couldn't wait to get back to Offley and begin work on this new and exciting project.

I read several books very quickly, I met people involved in training clowns, thought very hard, and finally produced around ten thousand words for the project I called 'Gospel Fool.' I had thought that the course would be a rest. As it turned out, it was to prove to be very much more.

I am so grateful to Bishop Peter Mumford for sending me on this course. He once told me that the only reason he had been kicked upstairs to be a bishop was he had made such a terrible mess of being an archdeacon. He must have got something right because he went on from St Albans Diocese to be Bishop of Truro. This time at Windsor was literally a Godsend. I don't remember too much about the study sessions. I do remember one, though, which was about people's models of the church. I was sitting in the back of the room, as any normal Anglican would. At the front, the warden of St George's House Professor Charles Handy was leading the session. At one point I was so bored with all the talk about models of the church, I got off my seat, walked to the front, and drew a picture on the flip chart. It was of a compost heap, steaming with the heat of the chemical reactions going on within it. There was a nearly exotic plant growing out of the top of the heap. 'There's my model of the church, a compost heap. On its own, it's of no bloody use at all and it probably stinks. Spread it around and all kinds of things begin to grow, or grow better,' I said and sat down. I think Charles Handy quite enjoyed the compost heap picture or model of the church for he spoke of it when being interviewed by the BBC's religious affairs correspondent, Gerald Priestland, in the series 'Priestland's Progress' for Radio 4, broadcast in the winter of 1981.

Between completing the Cambridge Radio Course in 1979 and going to the mid-service clergy course in July 1980, Chris Rees asked me if I would consider working as his researcher for a series of thirteen programmes on the Christian faith for BBC Radio 4. I generally say yes to things without thinking them through, but on this occasion I said no to Chris Rees. Local radio was coming to the diocese, I was finding that split jobs are never split fifty-fifty. Split jobs, I believe, are an abomination. In my case, I was priest in charge of two small country parishes, I was communications officer for the diocese though the diocese would probably have rather not had me. I was editor of the diocesan monthly paper, *See Round*. We were living in a marvellous large vicarage which we discovered was quite impossible to heat. In our first winter there we spent money on coal for the living room fire, oil for the central heating and hot water boiler, on Calor gas to warm the rooms the central heating couldn't or wouldn't heat, electricity for fan heaters for a freezing study.

Split jobs satisfy no-one. Split jobs are supposed to be half-time doing one job and half-time doing the other. Too easily they become two-thirds doing one job and two-thirds doing another. People find it difficult to come to terms with being less than another's full-time concern. Whenever you are wanted in one place, you are somewhere else. Split jobs need rethinking or abolishing. They are often the result of muddled thinking or no thought at all. I certainly helped Bishop Runcie with his communications. One day near Christmas in Offley and Lilley, his chaplain Richard Chartres rang me up to say that the Hemel Hempstead *Post Echo* newspaper had asked Bishop Runcie to write a Christmas piece for the newspaper. It was to be so many words long and the bishop would need it in ten days' time. I said that I had no idea what the bishop thought about Christmas but that I would have a go and he would have it by the deadline.

In fact, I was so unsure what the bishop thought about Christmas or what he might want to tell the readers of the *Post Echo* that I wrote two pieces, to give him a choice. I imagine he must have approved of one of them. Nobody complained.

When Robert Runcie was named as the next Archbishop of Canterbury his office was nearly overwhelmed by requests for interviews or articles and I was drawn in to draft some of these pieces. Two stick in my mind, one for *Scouting Today* and the other for *Vogue* magazine, a coincidence given that my mother had once worked for *Vogue* and had risen to being beauty editor for the magazine as well as editor of *Vogue Beauty Book*. Perhaps if I had gone with the Archbishop-designate to Canterbury and Lambeth, I might have made more inroads into the business of ghostwriting. Richard Chartres did ask me if I would like to move from St Albans down to London and Kent, but I thought it would not be a good idea. Selfishly I may have been beginning to think of writing a book about fools and clowns, and I didn't think that would have been possible or acceptable while working for the Archbishop in communications. I don't think I had a positive enough attitude towards authority to have lasted long at Lambeth or Canterbury.

To return to my debate with Chris Rees about working as researcher for the *Priestland* programmes, I discovered Chris Rees is a determined man. After my first refusal, he tried again sometime later. Again, I said no. More time passed, and presumably the need for a researcher remained. More time passed and, this is beginning to sound a bit biblical, he asked me yet a third time. I repeated, 'no!' He asked me why. 'I imagine you are looking for someone who is disciplined, neat and tidy in thought, word, and deed, thinks in straight lines, who is organized. I am none of these things.' 'I know that,' said Chris. 'Why do you think I keep asking you?' That was a bit of a clincher. I am sure at some point Chris said it would only involve some ten days of work and that he would ask the new Bishop of St Albans, John Bernard Taylor, for permission for me to do the work. The bishop said yes.

Priestland's Progress was a brilliant series. I had really no idea what my role would be, and it was fun finding out. I had a hand or a foot in the design of the series. I had read an interesting book about the teaching of theology at Harvard School of Divinity, *Christian Theology – A Case Study Approach*, by Parker and Evans. It seems that the divinity school had learned something new about teaching from the faculty of law. Once upon a time future lawyers learned law by rote. Only then were they encouraged to look at real cases. The faculty turned this process on its head and looked first at cases from real life, then went to see how the law might bear upon those cases. This reminded me of Mr Brock's way of teaching O level Maths at Westminster where he told gripping and enthralling stories within which he had folded the maths he wanted us to learn. The storytelling approach got me through the examination as no other teaching method could have done. Theology has been called the 'queen of sciences,' but sometimes the queen can seem to be at sixes and sevens with those who try to follow or understand her.

Harvard applied the law faculty stories-from-real-life approach in its teaching of divinity. This seemed to be an approach that might work with this series for Radio 4. Gerald, the consummate journalist with a love of the English language would travel in search of the truth of Christianity and the series would be an account of his journey, his story. We asked a team of four eminent churchmen – Bishop Stephen Neill of the Church of England, Bishop David Konstant of the Roman Catholic Church, Professor William Shaw of the Church of Scotland, and the Reverend Doctor Gordon Rupp of the Methodists – to set out the main themes which could be explored on Gerald's journey. We then had a team of four wise men, Anglican Archbishop Robert Runcie, Roman Catholic Cardinal Basil Hume, Methodist Lord Soper, and Bishop Lesslie Newbigin of the United Reformed Church to whom we could turn for expert questioning.

Once we had the themes in order, Hugh Faupel and I as researchers got down to listing people Gerald might interview, together with the subject areas to be covered, information about the interviewees and possible questions. The interview team consisted of Gerald Priestland, producer Chris Rees, a BBC sound engineer, and on occasions, me or Hugh. We ended up with around 100 interviews, mostly around thirty minutes each, to be distilled down into just thirteen forty-five-minute programmes.

Chris Rees insisted that at the end of each interview, Gerald and the interviewee sit in silence for three minutes while the sound engineer recorded the sound of the room. These inserts would be used to

Video interview about Priestland's Progrees in 2014

smooth the transitions from the sound of one set of surroundings to the next place of interview. Over time, these silences became much commented on by the interviewees themselves, nearly all of them opting to remain in the room and enjoy the silences, which were never completely silent. Gerald in his introduction to the BBC book of the series wrote, 'I mean no disrespect to their eloquence when I say that it was usually the best part of the interview.'

There was one occasion when I felt a complete spoilsport and we hadn't quite got to the silence. Gerald was interviewing Captain Christine Parkin of the Salvation Army in Bedford. Gerald asked me if I thought we had what we needed, and I said I thought he should ask Christine about prayer. The interview resumed and she told a really moving story she had told me weeks and weeks before. It concerned her son who was suffering from eczema. Specialists and experts had been seen and Christine was almost at the end of her rope. One night as she put her son to bed, she prayed, put everything in God's hands, saying she could not do any more, it was up to God. And from that moment her son began to get better. It was a powerful story.

Thinking back, I don't think anyone else could have handled as Gerald did being both the subject of the story and object of the series. One of my tasks once the series began to be broadcast late on Sunday nights, repeated on a weekday afternoon, was to read all the letters from listeners. Gerald knew that some would require a personal and pastoral letter which he would write himself. By the time I left working on the series, I think I had read some seventeen thousand of the twenty-two thousand letters received. We had a whole shelf of little blue books which listeners had sent us in order to set us straight in our understanding of Christian doctrine, prayer, and worship. That said, most of the letters were complimentary, we had very few abusive ones. The audience at that time on a Sunday night was multiplied by a factor of four times, audience research showed. Years later, walking away from Broadcasting House, having contributed a live 'Pause for Thought' on Radio 2, the producer asked me if I had been involved in *Priestland's Progress*. I said I had, and he told me that he had rushed home from college to hear the weekday afternoon repeats, and the series had convinced him he should become a religious programmes producer. Chris Rees tells me he has heard from up to ten listeners who offered for ordination to the priesthood as a result of listening to the programmes.

While we were still making the programmes, I was asked to write study notes for house or church groups who might be using the series to broaden their understanding and discuss what they had heard. This was the first time I had ever tried to write such a thing and it was another writing challenge.

Before all the programmes were completed, Chris Rees asked me if I would finally shorten two of the programmes as he needed to take some time off on holiday to recover from the strains and stresses of it all. He was not only responsible for this series but for *Good Morning Sunday* on Radio 2. This was a challenge as these were programmes which Gerald and Chris had agreed said all they wanted to say but were too long for the broadcast slot. One needed nearly eight minutes taken out of it, the other one between three and four minutes. I found a quiet corner and with a stopwatch and a pair of headphones listened to the programmes several times over a couple of days. I made copious notes: 'three seconds from here, he's said that twice, he didn't need to, let's take that out.'

Eventually I booked an editing studio in Broadcasting House with a studio manager who edited the programmes at my direction. Producers, never mind lowly temporary researchers, would be fired if they were caught editing programme tapes. All was going well until, with one edit, the studio manager said, 'You can't do that there.' I asked him why, then told him to make the edit. He did. It worked.

I must have got something right as at the end of the session both the programmes were the correct length, and Chris on his return from holiday told me he could not tell where I had made the edits.

I was paid £10 a day for my work as a researcher and, in that curious BBC way, I was given a contract for ten days work at a time after I had done it and asked to sign it so that I could be paid. Inevitably there were many more days than the ten Chris had stipulated when he finally succeeded in getting me to agree to do the work and permission from my bishop. While I was working on *Priestland's Progress,* I became drawn into leading the *Daily Service* on Radio 4. This was a privilege and an interesting encounter with live broadcasting. All the hymns and readings were chosen and set by the programme's producer. All I had to do was to attend the rehearsal beforehand with the BBC Singers, time the hymn verses with a stopwatch, and make sure that everything ran to time with the broadcast itself, generally from All Souls, Langham Place. I had been warned that at any moment, I might hear in one side of my headphones that I would have to end a minute or a half early because a gale warning or some other important words had to be broadcast before the time signal and news at 11 a.m. Because I knew how long hymn verses had taken at rehearsal, I would then decide quickly what would need to be cut and semaphore to the director of the singers. It was strange keeping one ear on the service as being broadcast, keeping one ear open for any sudden request from continuity, while being aware of underground trains far beneath the church on their way to or from Oxford Circus, buses or ambulances passing outside the church.

It was about this time that I wondered whether I should be working in religious broadcasting full time. I have somewhere a copy of a job application for a production job for the BBC. Nothing came of it. Probably just as well. It was good that the series received a Sandford St Martin Trust award. Gerald generously shared the award with the programme team, and we went to a great awards lunch in Lambeth Palace on 7 June 1982. I was seated next to Gerald who sat next to the chairman of the BBC governors. At one point, the chairman remarked to Gerald how difficult he found it getting servants. I couldn't resist saying to Gerald, 'You know, I have exactly the same problem.' Gerald whispered that I should wave goodbye to any thoughts of working for the BBC.

CHAPTER 13

Me, a clown?

As a result of the paper 'Gospel Fool' and the contacts I had made while writing it, chiefly clown priest Roly Bain, trainer of clowns Carole Crowther, and others, I was being drawn into the possibility of helping to put together a group called Holy Fools in this country.

I was invited to take Annette and Stephen to the annual Clown, Mime/Puppet, Dance and Storytelling Ministry workshop over a week at the American University in Washington, DC. Our airfares were covered and accommodation and meals at the workshop were exchanged for just two lectures I was asked to do. This conference was an eye opener. Across the United States at that time there were some three thousand clown ministry groups, and at the conference there were many movers and shakers from these ministries. There were lectures and workshops, and some exercises. I was involved at one point in a clown and politics workshop. One of the major political issues at the time was the proposed development of a very clever nuclear bomb, the neutron bomb, which, it was said, would be of great value as it would just kill people while leaving buildings and infrastructure still standing. I suppose you could see it as the perfect capitalist weapon. We had to decide what clowning could say to this situation.

In the end after much discussion and the fashioning of some props we met just outside the White House railings, all dressed in clown and stopping passers-by and asking them if they had heard of this wonderful new technology. We told them about proposed refinements, a colour neutron bomb that would be skin-colour sensitive, leaving all the blacks alive while killing all the whites, or the religious versions which would, say, kill Protestants while leaving Catholics alive.

Then we organized an arms race, lining up the competitors, setting them to run to the finish line. We all crowded round the winner as he opened his beautifully gift-wrapped prize. Beneath the sparkly wrapping paper and bows, there was a beautiful box. The lid was removed, and the winner found a small cone of ashes. It was quite a powerful moment.

I am sure we aroused the curiosity of the different police forces – the White House Police, the Washington Parks Police, and who knows how many members of the FBI. Every morning began with worship. One day this was led by one of the organizing staff. He took us through the genealogy at the start of Matthew's gospel. As he read out each name in the family tree, he held up placards – one Hurrah! for the heroes, one Boo! for the villains, and one with a giant question mark suggesting we knew almost nothing about the name he had just mentioned. I doubt any bunch of Christians has ever listened so carefully to a gospel genealogy with so much interest, laughter, and enjoyment.

I met a lovely clown minister from California, Doug Adams, associate professor at the Pacific School of Religion, Berkeley. He told me about one of the groups of students there. 'We have a Body and Soul company and they work in therapeutic settings, in children's homes, mental hospitals, and a number of convalescent homes and homes for the elderly. Touching is so important there. People aren't touched enough particularly when they're older and when they're children.'

'We had one child in a children's home, he was really only about one year old, and because we had been working there some time we got a call and they asked if some of our clowns would come over just to hold this child. This child had just been dropped off at the home. He had never been touched by his parents. He had no visible emotions and they simply wanted us to hold and fondle that child for three months running. Our clowns are used to touching, so they agreed. A bunch of them went over there with some of the dancers who appreciated that need, and they took turns. At the end of three months, the child smiled for the first time.'

'People may not be able to hear, they may even be senile or what we call senile, but the thing that they have at the end is the sense of touch. They often have a sense of colour too. When we go to work in these homes, we don't want to work with those who are mobile. We want to work with the ones they don't normally bring out, the ones they call senile. We can communicate with them through touch, through movement and colour, the things which clowns and dancers bring.'

I asked what effect this had on his students. 'When they begin to value elements of people who don't have other qualities, when they begin to value the qualities of people even though they cannot speak properly, even though they cannot constrain their own emotions very well, then they begin to value the qualities in themselves and in other people, not just those who are institutionalised. So, I find that these students become whole persons themselves. They begin to find things in themselves that they have suppressed. Often in our classes people will come out and say, 'Well, there are three brilliant students, but I can do without the rest.' They come out of those classes after the experience in children's homes and the convalescent homes learning that there's something to be learnt in each person whether they are brilliant or not. And to me that's a major piece of learning especially in the Church. God help us if they only value the few that are brilliant in the Church.'

Dave Mura, a Roman Catholic priest from the Diocese of Rochester, New York, got into clowning through a friend who had been to a Holy Fools for Christ's Sake workshop. 'I decided I could be a clown; it was a good way of turning on the kids in our parish. So, we put on the makeup, we put it on all wrong. We went out to a nursing home, did all the wrong things but had a good time. We came back and started doing some more, went to the workshop in Nashville and just took off from there. The one thing that clowning provides is a non-threatening way for kids to deal with old people and sick people. They can sort of hide behind the mask. Once they realize that mask is the means of reaching the old people they just get thrilled by the whole thing. Kids are so often rejected because they are just kids. They can put on a clown face and be immediately accepted. I've seen in many cases that even after they've got out of clown they've gained, through the hiding, an understanding of old and sick people. Then they can take off the mask and continue doing the same.'

And they have clearly gained a clearer understanding of themselves through clowning. 'They say, "Gee, I've got something in me that I can give to somebody else." As kids we are often told, "You're too young" or "You don't know enough" or "We've tried that before," whereas, when a kid can put on a clown and give himself to somebody, he says, "Who cares if you tried it before, it's still working!"' Dave Mura's kids then, were finding their way into clowning, and in doing so, found that they could relate to old and sick people, that they had someone, something to give . . . the gift of themselves.

I also met Margie Brown, a member of the United Methodist Church, commissioned by her church to an itinerant ministry of storytelling. She suffered from cerebral palsy and had worked as a circus clown. For her the Bible is a book of questions, not of answers. 'If you tell people the answers, they file them away somewhere and forget about them. If you ask them to ask the questions, then they will have the joy of finding their own answers. I fear that too much church is made up of people telling others the answers to questions they haven't begun to ask.'

Jesus taught by telling stories, leaving his hearers to ask the question, 'What's this story about?' Rabbis tell stories. If you ask them what they are about, you don't get an answer making everything clear, you get another story which you will have to work on to find out the answer or even more questions.

While in the United States we visited friends in Texas. They had arranged for me to preach at a United Methodist Church in Arlington. We found the church, it had an enormous car park and was superbly staffed and equipped. No-one had told me I would be preaching at three services, one after the other. I was moved by their habit of all standing up and reading from the Bible together.

Inevitably when we got home and told people about our experiences in Washington, the question arose as to whether some sort of Holy Fools UK group might be established, learning from what had been developed across America. Several of us got together and talked this through and eventually decided yes, that there should be Holy Fools in this country, and, yes, that there should be a clown, mime, puppet, dance, and storytelling workshop, to which the Americans promised they would send over some hundreds of participants. Naively we went ahead and booked Southlands College in Wimbledon for a fortnight. A few of us, including Roly Bain, Carole Crowther of Clown Cavalcade, clown and fire-eating storyteller Sandra Pollerman, worked hard at planning a programme and invited people to lead workshops.

To cut a long story short, we suddenly heard from the US that no-one would be coming despite their promises and commitment. I talked to Southlands who promptly sent me an invoice for thousands of pounds in cancellation fees. I wrote back and said that they should forward it to the people who had committed to bringing hundreds of Americans across the Atlantic and had clearly not delivered.

Desperate to mount some sort of substitute gathering we were invited to use St James' Church, Piccadilly for a weekend workshop in 1983. Some sixty people came for the weekend which culminated in a parish Eucharist, with clowning, dance, and a sermon from Roly Bain. A bishop, I think it was Bishop David Sheppard, who had dropped in unannounced to join the congregation said afterwards that it was one of the most moving and reverent services he had ever attended.

Holy Fools UK was formed, very loosely, and still exists. I particularly remember invitations to perform in hospitals and prisons. It was in Wandsworth Prison that I discovered both the joy and terror of improvisation. Living on the edge of Bedfordshire and up to my neck in parish, diocese, and local radio, it made no sense to travel to London to rehearse with the others who would visit the prison. So, I suggested they give me a slot of a few minutes which I would try to fill in as clowning a way as I could imagine.

Sandra Pollerman had been doing some fire-eating and she asked me to cross the stage to fetch her a glass of water from the tiny room which served as a vestry for the prison chapel where we were performing. I found a glass, filled it with cold water. My eye was caught by a bucket beneath the wash hand basin. I don't know why but I put the glass of water for Sandra in the bucket and walked back across the stage. As I did so, the prisoners started to laugh.

When it came to my slot in the programme, I walked on stage in my clown shoes, trousers and shirt, makeup and wig. I took the bucket with me, and simply improvised the seven ages of bucket clown. I said nothing. I began as a small child sitting on the potty, straining. Then I became a toddler playing soldiers with the bucket. The more I did, the more the prisoners laughed. Afterwards, once we had been released to go to the pub, I sat down and asked the others what all this bucket stuff had been about. 'You fool,' they said, which I took as a compliment, 'can't you see, you were helping them to laugh at something that is profoundly awful and un-funny, the business of having no access to the loo during the night hours. You have a bucket in your cell and whatever is in it in the morning has to be slopped out.' I should have seen this, having been a prison visitor in my last year and three months at Lincoln. Clearly if something dreadful can be laughed at it loses its power over you. Which takes me straight back to the medieval joke about death: Death enters and Everyman looks up at him and says, 'Ah, Death, I thought you'd be thinner!' Laugh at death and death loses his power.

Improvisation is a sort of discipline I try to embrace. Part of this is undoubtedly because I am rubbish at learning lines. I have been to courses teaching improv but there's a bit of me that thinks improvisation is best learned on the job. Once I was asked to go to an evening service marking the fifth birthday of the Barnes Fools in South London. I arrived good and early and was asked where I wanted to be when preaching the sermon I had carefully crafted. I asked what locations were on offer and was told that the chancel step or the pulpit were available. So far, so boring, I thought. 'Oh, and there's a portable lectern you might like to use.' I had never seen one of these but it's a sort of ecclesiastical invention based on the humble deck chair. Instead of the long piece of canvas favoured by the deck chair there is a strip of leather which when extended should accommodate a preacher's notes or script. I looked at this thing and said that it would do very nicely. When the moment came to preach, I went to fetch this object and then spent some four minutes or so playing with it and trying to make it work. By the time I had wrestled it into use, the curate was laughing so much that he had to leave the building, his stomach hurting from laughter. After that introduction, I think I could have honestly preached that black was white, which of course it is. I was quietly thrilled and thankful that it had been such an unexpected gift to all of us there.

Roly Bain was vicar of St Paul's Furzedown, and when I had written my first book, *Gospel of Folly*, published in 1988, the front cover was a picture I had taken of Roly giving the chalice to a communicant while dressed not in ecclesiastical garb but in his clown costume. It's a great picture but it did the book no favours as I was told that a few Christian bookshops wouldn't handle the book as they believed the front cover to be blasphemous. Oh dear. A further unhelpful opinion came from the then Bishop of Edinburgh, Richard Holloway who damned the book when asked to review it in the *Church Times*. Talking to Susan Young, the news editor, she told me she was embarrassed for they hoped that book reviewers if they did not like a book would at least try to imagine who would and recommend it to them. Asked about it some years later the good bishop conceded that perhaps he had been a bit hard on me. The book made no money, but I had to write it, if only for myself, though some readers enjoyed it.

A book that was published the same year was *Vicar's World* written by Canon Bill Ritson and me, published by Jarrolds of Norwich. Dendle French was the parish priest in Whitwell and his daughter Liz asked him if he knew of someone who might write a humorous A-to-Z about the church. Dendle told her about me. I thought I would like to write it, but I would rather co-write it and thought of Bill Ritson who worked at St Albans Abbey. We both went to Norwich to meet Jarrolds and got the job. Jarrolds were going to publish four humorous books in time for Christmas. One was to be about politics, one about restaurants, one about horse racing, and the fourth about the Church. They were to be paperbacks, modestly priced and suitable to put in Auntie Rotter's Christmas stocking without the chance of her being offended.

We divided up the alphabet between us, and what we did not know we either looked up or made up. The book went off like a rocket, the print run of 7,000 sold out, and Bill and I received £1,400 each. He had never been to Florence so went on holiday there, and I paid off a lot of bills.

Clowns and fools, storytelling, mime, puppetry, and dance have such a contribution to make to the life and work and worship of the church, there is not enough time or space to explore it fully here. In 1995 Roly Bain and I put together a handbook for aspiring holy fools and clowns for Church House Publishing. We called it *Clowning Glory*, and for the cover a friend, Rachel Morton, took a picture of Roly and me on the roof of Church House, both in clown gear, Roly with the Bible and me with a trombone which I was trying to learn. The book is still available.

After Roly had been in his parish for six years he decided to train as a clown at Fool Time, a circus school in Bristol. So, he took a year out and developed his clowning skills to professional standards. He discovered that he was a 'natural' on the slack rope and this became his signature skill in addition to a winsome ability to get away with custard pie-ing bishops of the Church of England.

The Holy Fools have been asked to all manner of events. One I remember was a conference of prison chaplains. It was held on the campus of Nottingham University. We were asked to take part in the conference service. The main procession with a bishop or two and the choir lined up to move into the church. The Holy Fools were lurking around the vestry and I suggested we follow the main procession. A crucifer held high a processional cross, and I looked around for something to carry. I found a filthy mop with a long handle, raised it high and we walked into the church. Was I imagining it or was there really a sense of the mood lightening as we drew level with the chaplains as they stood in their places, a sense that maybe this service wasn't going to be as it had always been down the years?

At the conference dinner, I suggested that the fools help serve the meal and I quickly learned how to balance maybe four dinners on my arms ready to serve to the conference members. Afterwards at the conference entertainment, I performed a variation of my prison bucket routine and with the bucket firmly over my head and unable to see a thing, I ended up sitting in the Lady Mayoress's lap.

To enable Roly to explore his clowning ministry, the Faith and Foolishness Trust was established to secure grants, to publicise Roly's work and to support and encourage him in any way we could. His was an amazing piece of work. He notched up thousands of miles visiting prisons, hospitals, schools, churches. The trust ensured that Roly received regular annual health checks, tried to fund a replacement when he wore out his car. Roly's death saddened the Holy Fools. He was our standard-bearer and I believe the church has lost a pioneer in the ministry which clowns and fools can serve.

CHAPTER 14

The bad Samaritan

My time in St Albans Diocese was a kaleidoscopic mixture or muddle of so many elements that it was no surprise to me when it began to implode. A typical Sunday would start with me getting up around five o'clock, crossing the road to the church to wind the clock in the church tower, switch on the largely ineffective electric water boiler for the radiators, then drive quickly to Chiltern Radio in Dunstable, where I unlocked the doors, took the station out of its overnight pre-recorded programme mode and put on a half-hour programme, farming based, in the early years. Our programme *Travelling* started at 7 a.m. and ran until 8.30 a.m. Then it was back on the road to Lilley to take the Communion service at 9.30, before driving up the hill to Great Offley to take their Communion service at 11 a.m. By lunch time, I was beginning to feel like an out-of-sorts bear. In the evening there was either evensong at St Mary Magdalene Church or a service at the Methodist Chapel.

Early one Sunday morning I was driving out of Great Offley when I saw a figure lying by the side of the road. I thought it was a tramp rough sleeping and went on my way. Later I found out that it was a villager who had come off his friend's motorcycle around midnight when it crashed into a concrete bollard. I think the friend was killed outright, and his pillion rider, the man I saw on the grass verge, was taken to hospital where he eventually died of his injuries. I visited him in hospital where they could do nothing for him.

I felt that I had failed this man and his wife and family. It was a Bad Samaritan story. In the gospel I am sure that the priest and the Levite were torn by their duties and the conventions of religious purity but followed them rather than help the man who fell among thieves. On other occasions I have stopped to give whatever assistance I could, but on this day I passed the man too quickly to discern his situation, and anyway I was due to open Chiltern Radio, only I had the keys, and there was a programme to present or produce.

I know others have managed the twin responsibilities of being a parish priest as well as fulfilling religious broadcasting commitments, but these two sets of obligations had collided for me and raised the question of whether I could do both. I am fairly certain that the man had been so severely injured and had lain where he was for so long that even if I had stopped, raised the alarm, he was beyond medical assistance, but I don't know for sure. Having visited the man in hospital, I took the funeral for the family and confessed to his widow that I had driven past her husband without realizing what the situation was.

At the meeting of Bishop's Council where my working full time in communications was considered, I was asked during a coffee break if I would miss the altar. This was a question I had not heard or thought about and I am not sure how I answered. I was aware that the diocese probably didn't think too much about communications. I had been sent to all the deanery synods to talk about communications and why they mattered. There were always some angry questions about my work in religious broadcasting. Why, I was asked, did Travelling go out at a time when many of them would be in church? I usually answered that I had no say in when broadcasts were scheduled and added that maybe the programmes were not for them as they were already inside the church. Back would come another question. What are all these Muslims, Jews, Sikhs, Hindus, Bahais doing in your programme? I explained that I was involved in religious broadcasting, responsible for reflecting the breadth of religious experience and practice in the audience area. I added that what we were engaged in was pre-evangelism, telling stories, illustrating what the various faiths were about. I was not allowed by broadcasting law to evangelise. That was their job, the work of the local church. I sensed they were not best pleased with my answers.

I did from time to time however bump into people who were listeners to *Travelling*. I was preaching one Sunday in a church in Hitchin, and a man came up to me as he was leaving the church, asking me if I was involved with Chiltern Radio's *Travelling*. I said I was, and he told me that listening to the programme had led to his returning to church. Mercifully, such encounters have been very rare. Mercifully, because it would be hard to avoid a certain swelling of the head at the thought of listeners having their lives altered in any way. It is significant that most thoughtful broadcasters and preachers admit that they know that they are talking to just one listener.

Almost all my time with radio has been to do with telling stories, asking questions. Time and again in local radio we would hear of something interesting happening in a parish. I would ring up and ask if someone would be prepared to be interviewed. The response would generally be, 'You need to talk to the priest or the minister.' I would then persist and say that I could fill the programme end to end with bishops, clergy, ministers, returning missionaries and what would be the result? People would think only the professionals could handle the faith and if that were the case the faith was doomed. Again and again, we proved that people could perfectly well tell stories themselves in an interesting and engaging way. The discovery or recovery of nerve or competence matters more than I can say and is wonderful to behold when it happens.

'Thoughts for the Day' were also opportunities for people to write what they thought or believed and then record what they had written. I was very moved by a contributor who had sent in some really good scripts but who rang up and said that he thought that once I had heard his voice, I might like to get someone else to voice what he had written. I insisted that this was local radio and that I should record him delivering them himself. He did. They were broadcast and two presenters at the radio station offered diametrically opposite opinions. One more experienced presenter said he thought the contributor was very brave to deliver his thoughts. The other, more ambitious and pushier, once asked why on earth I had let him on air with a voice like that. Years later towards the end of our time at Chiltern, that last presenter decided one day that he didn't like a thought which had been contributed by a remarkable nun from a community in Harpenden and, very unprofessionally, he stopped the piece halfway through being broadcast, rather like the priest who halted a funeral eulogy halfway through. I was listening at home and, furious, drove to Dunstable and told the presenter that he should never have done such a thing. I went to the nun, explained what had happened and apologized profusely for the presenter's unprofessionalism. After that event, rather than hazard contributors' pieces, I wrote and recorded all the 'Thoughts for the Day' myself until the day the team walked out of Chiltern Radio for good.

Our relationships with management at Chiltern were fraught from time to time. These were the Thatcher years and one day I had broadcast a 'Thought for the Day' and the programme controller said he thought it was 'a bit political.' I had quoted a news story in which it had been claimed that the rich were getting richer and the poor were getting poorer. I quoted my source to the programme controller and that was the end of the matter.

One year I was preparing our Good Friday special which we had broadcast since the station opened. For months if not years I had been trying to get the Roman Catholic Bishop of Northampton to contribute to our programmes and he had finally written and recorded a particularly good meditation for Good Friday. A few days before Good Friday I was called in to see the managing director and his programme controller. They told me that there would not be a Good Friday special programme that year. I asked why. 'Our listeners want pop music and shopping on Good Friday,' I was told. I asked what they thought I should say by way of explanation to the Roman Catholic bishop. They had no answer but eventually suggested I could use the material I had recorded and arranged for Good Friday in our programme on Easter Day. Gritting my teeth, I drew their attention to the difference between Good Friday and Easter. I could not change their minds, so I had to write to the Bishop of Northampton to explain why his piece or any of our material for Good Friday had not been broadcast.

Things were not all bad at Chiltern. Each year we would broadcast a special from the Christian Arts Festival, Greenbelt. These broadcasts were great fun as there were so many interesting people gathered in one place. I have mentioned the occasion when our generator cutting out during a commercial break went a long way to proving the existence of God. Barry and I discovered the therapeutic properties of whisky at nine o'clock on a Sunday morning. On another occasion, I was at Dunstable putting in the commercials and the records for our Greenbelt programme. The BT line, which connected us in the studio in Dunstable to the outside broadcast unit at Castle Ashby where Greenbelt was being held, had been booked from, I think, 6.30 a.m. I was in at Chiltern radio by 6 a.m. as usual that morning. I looked for the BT line at 6.30. Nothing. At 6.45, I tried again, still no line. At seven o'clock, there was still no line. So I started the programme, welcoming people and telling them that we would be crossing to Greenbelt after some music. Fortunately, I had the music for the programme while all the taped interviews and guests were with the outside broadcast unit. I put on the first two records, and the line came up during the first commercial break. Later we heard that the broadcast line went from Castle Ashby to Birmingham, to London, to Luton and Dunstable, and someone somewhere had not put the right plug in place or neglected to pull some switch or other. Chiltern may have been invoiced for this line, but I believe the bill was never paid and the reason for non-payment was strenuously stated.

For a little while I was a member of the share-owning plutocracy. On a whim I had bought fifty shares in Chiltern Radio. This enabled me to go to annual meetings of the company, usually held in Bedford where I was able to mischievously argue for more money for religious broadcasting. As a ploy it didn't work, much as I expected. However, as years went by, the shares were added to, became more valuable and there was a bid for the company. I received a letter from Chiltern asking me not to sell. Eventually I did, and, wonder of wonders, my original £50 worth became worth some £1,400.

In 1987, six years after we began broadcasting with Chiltern radio, I was visiting their Northampton office. The programme controller said that he was glad to see me as he had some news for me. *Travelling* was to start, not at 7 a.m. as it had for six years, but at 6 a.m. I knew from Rajar audience figures that at 6 a.m., the audience was a quarter of what it was at 7 a.m. I thought that this was scant reward for all the hard work we had put in over the years: *Travelling*, Lent courses and documentaries, 'Thoughts for the Day.' I said I thought that the team would not be happy at this development. I was right.

We took almost no time to agree that this change was unacceptable. We contacted the church leaders and the Radio Committee, and they made it very clear that unless the decision was reversed, they would withdraw the team from the radio station and told Chiltern so.

Meanwhile, I went to see the director of Religious Broadcasting at the Independent Broadcasting Authority, Eric Shegog, whom I had last met when he was vicar of St Michael and All Angels, across the level crossing at Abbey Wood in South London. I explained what had happened at Chiltern, what the team and I thought about it, and what the church leaders proposed to do. I think he was horrified not at what Chiltern had decided but at our readiness to walk away from the radio station and all its opportunities.

I learned later that Chiltern were extremely angry that I had been to the IBA as they were caught changing the timing of a religious programme without the required notification to the IBA.

CHAPTER 15

BBC Bedfordshire to Church House

The team moved to BBC Radio Bedfordshire (now BBC Three Counties Radio) and became responsible for their Sunday morning religious magazine programme, *Melting Pot*. Moving to the BBC was great. We found a management who better understood what religious broadcasting was about. The managing editor, Mike Gibbons, played the church organ in the village where he lived in Bedfordshire and told me once that he listened to our programme on headphones while sitting at the organ keyboard. He certainly knew the difference between Good Friday and Easter. We didn't miss the interruptions of commercial breaks. And all the music we played was logged by computer bar codes.

Because we were responsible for religious broadcasting, we were sent all manner of books and records from companies anxious to push their products. We used a minimum of the music we were sent. We were critical of the quality and I confess that we offered many of the records we didn't much like and would not play as prizes to listeners. While at Chiltern, I had once been rung up in my St Albans office by London Weekend Television who were keen to feature a new product, walk on water technology, inflatable skis which would enable us to literally walk across water. Could I find one or two other clergy who would be prepared to put on cassocks and race across St Katharine Dock in London? I contacted a couple of priests I thought would volunteer and we practised putting on these skis and carefully walking on water. Came the programme, hosted by Michael Aspel, and we raced across the Dock. I think I won but the director had asked that whoever won we should all contrive to fall in at the end of the race. It wasn't difficult. We dried out and spent an interesting hour or two on the boat which was being used in the programme. Days later I rang the company responsible for these things and asked if I could have a pair to give away to a listener to *Travelling*. They duly arrived and one listener was delighted to receive the prize. I did suggest that they were not used by children, and not in the sea.

It was wonderfully stretching to be so involved in local radio. Most radio listeners listen on their own. Radio is a magical medium for telling stories and storytelling is an art that from time to time threatens to disappear. Yet without the gift and art of storytelling there would be no gospel, no church, little faith, and much unbelief. One year while still at Chiltern Radio, we decided to produce a Lent course looking at the main claims and practices of the different faiths represented in our area. As if that wasn't ambitious enough, we thought what fun it might be to get different groups of students from Luton Sixth Form College to make half-hour programmes about their faiths. I had to explain that the programmes were not about converting listeners from one faith or no faith to the programme makers' faith. We showed the students how to interview, how to choose or reject what contributors might say. The last programme in the series was to be by a group of Muslim students. The difficulties of arranging for everyone concerned to meet resulted in a final editing and assembly of the programme on the afternoon of the day on which it was to be broadcast in the evening.

Some of the students were late when I drove to collect them at the College. It was snowing and, perhaps reacting to a full load of students, my Citroen 2CV chose that day to have a puncture halfway to Dunstable. I swapped the offending wheel for the spare and we finally arrived at the studios.

I was still editing the second half of the programme as the first half was being broadcast. During the commercial break between the two halves, I as near as anything collapsed with the stress of it all. It was certainly the nearest I ever came to walking right out of radio. I'm glad I didn't. The programme was broadcast with perhaps one dud edit in it, which with any luck few would have noticed.

It was perhaps time for a rest from broadcasting. In 1990 I applied for the post of information officer in the communications unit at Church House in London headed by Eric Shegog. I was short-listed and called for an interview on a Friday afternoon. I worked on the programme *Melting Pot* at BBC Bedfordshire in Luton, drove home to Lilley for lunch. Annette greeted me with the news that she had looked at one of two suits I possessed. 'You can't wear your suit, it's so old it has flares. I've found one your brother Mike handed down to you. I have shortened the waist and pressed the suit, wear that one.' I did as I was told, put on Mike's suit, and travelled by train to London. I walked along Victoria Street to Dean's Yard and Church House.

I was asked by one of the panel how I would feel about having to wear a suit to work. Whoever it was who asked the question must have known that I would generally only be seen in a suit on the rarest of occasions, my wedding or even my funeral. I answered by telling what I have just written that my one suit was too out of date with flares, and how I was wearing my older brother's suit. 'As I walked along Victoria Street, it didn't feel too bad and by the time I got to Dean's Yard, it almost felt alright, even possible,' I said. Among many other questions, I was asked how I would cope with fellow workers in Church House with whom I might find myself at odds. I said that I thought that there were probably people there whose necks I might cheerfully wring until their teeth rattled. I left the interview feeling I had done what I could.

It was a challenge for Bishop John Taylor, who was my bishop, and who was also chair of the Committee for Communications at Church House. Years earlier he had told me he was being asked to be the chairman of that committee, did I think he should take it. I said he should on one condition. That he should give something else up first to allow him to do the job well. I once offered to be his chaplain . . . on one condition, that I should also be his fool. He didn't bite.

He once told me earlier that I was a difficult person to place. I misinterpreted him as saying that I was just difficult. What he meant, he explained years later, was that it was difficult to place me somewhere where my gifts might be employed. A year or two earlier I had been summoned to meet the Bishop and Archdeacon of Bedford. When I arrived, I was asked how old I was, and what did I think I should do next after being communications officer. I said that I thought if they wanted to destroy a parish, they might put me in charge. I really wanted something to build on whatever skills or talents I might have acquired or developed. I heard no more from them. I think that was the closest I ever got to career or pastoral guidance from the institutional church.

The interview must have gone well because Anne Holt, the chief personnel officer at Church House, rang me at home at about eight o'clock that evening to offer me the post. I nearly could not believe it. I then discovered that the salary I would be paid as an ecclesiastical civil servant would be enough to pay the mortgage on 14 East Street, Lilley, which was owned by the diocese whose employment, for want of a better word, I was leaving.

At Church House, I was given a contract for four years' employment with the possibility of a negotiated renewal at the end of the four years, in 1995. There was also an arrangement by which I could have the money needed for an annual railway season ticket between Luton and St Pancras stations, with the money being deducted each month from my salary – salary, not stipend. In no time at all, we had negotiated to buy 14 East Street from the diocese. For some thirty thousand pounds more than they had paid for it. I discovered that I was buying the greenhouse I had bought and put in the garden for the second time. We were keen to stay where we were among friends we had got to know over the last twelve years. We had our feet in the housing market again and I found I was able to afford to buy CDs, mostly of classical music, which come into their own later in this story.

Church House rang me before I started working there to ask if I could come and meet a possible secretary. Of course, I would, I said. This was so different an approach from when I had joined St Albans Diocese, I almost fell off my perch with excitement. I travelled up to

London and was introduced to Denise Woodford who had worked for the Ministry of Defence and for the Soldiers, Sailors, Airmen and Families Association, SSAFA. Aside from asking her what her experience had been, where she had worked, there was only one question to be answered. Did she feel able to take me on and keep the inevitable paperwork and stuff around me sorted and accessible and cope with my pathological untidiness and flow of ideas? She thought for a moment and said she would like to try. The deal was done, and we started within days of one another in 1991.

Denise was a lifesaver. When we started, I was put into an office on the Communications corridor, I think, on the third floor. Quite soon most of the offices were put together in an open plan arrangement with Steve Jenkins, the press officer who had worked in journalism. Before he came to Church House he had been the press officer for The Children's Society. He and I sat facing each other. Denise sat at the desk facing my back, my best side. Other members of the unit were Eric's secretary Andrina Barnden, Steve Jenkins' assistant Alison Brand, and Steve Empson of the Church of England Enquiry Centre.

We installed and set up equipment which would automatically record BBC Radio 4 and Radio 2's output from 7 a.m. until 9 a.m., so that if there was something involving the Church of England, we could quickly access it and make it available to any senior bishops who might be questioned about it. We also installed a fresh coffee maker to help people to feel welcome to the unit. We served the best fair-trade coffee in the building. Hospitality has its place in good communications.

We also read all the daily newspapers for anything that might need an official response. For most of the time I worked at Church House, I chose to do this as I didn't mind being in the office by 8 a.m. Anything relevant would be cut out, copied, and faxed to all the bishops in the hope that if interviewed or questioned about any such story, they would be ready and briefed. I did ask one day whether I might leave a compensating hour early, say at four o'clock. No, I was very firmly told, you may not. It was worth asking, though. On Fridays I also read all the religious weekly papers, *The Church Times*, *The Church of England Newspaper*, the *Methodist Recorder*. I don't think we read the *Jewish Chronicle*. The experience of reading the church newspapers week by week was such that I vowed that when I retired, I would never read them again. So far, I have managed to keep that vow.

The unit was keen to train clergy and others in the wonders and mysteries of being interviewed on radio or writing for radio. For this we needed a state-of-the-art modern radio studio which would accurately reflect broadcasting reality. One of my earliest tasks was to get such a thing designed and built. A generous grant or two helped pay the £30,000 bill for this. The main contractors were a firm called Clyde Broadcast and they did a fine job of building an air-conditioned studio and control room, physically insulated from all the noises of Church House.

So now we had a studio which had an ISDN line, Integrated Services Digital Network or It Still Does Nothing, depending on whom you ask, a broadcast quality telephone line. At one point I was asked by Transworld Radio to broadcast a short early morning programme of music while some work was done on their studios. On one occasion the Princess Royal was in the building and needed to speak into *Woman's Hour* on Radio 4. A couple of days before the broadcast, officers of the Metropolitan Police Royalty Protection unit visited the studio with a sniffer dog to check for explosives in advance of the broadcast. They found nothing and I am glad to say that everything worked as it should have done.

Whenever there was a visitor in Church House who I thought might be of interest to local radio religious programme producers, I would either record an interview and fax the stations to say it was available if they wanted to download it via ISDN, or if the visitor was willing, arrange an interview down the line to them. There is no doubt in my mind that the studio was a great asset, both for training and for broadcast use. I would bet that people who came to be trained in being interviewed and writing 'Thoughts for the Day' would have learned a lot about the business of preaching. Grab the listener's attention, keep holding it with short sentences, great stories, marvellous scenery, and don't worry too much about punctuation.

This was the first office I had worked in where computers were part of the deal. At St Albans, there were no computers in the diocesan office on Holywell Hill except for a specialised piece of gear which handled the diocesan accounting. While at Lilley I had bought one of the first Amstrad computers, a CPC64 machine with coloured keys on its keyboard. I wrote my first book, *Gospel of Folly*, during a three-month sabbatical in 1987–1988 using this quite primitive computer with a word processing programme called Locoscript. I took it into St Albans one day and in no time at all, my office was the place to visit to see the technology wonder of the age. It was a brilliant introduction to computing and word processing, though I think 64 kilobits was the limit of its storage capacity. A cassette was built into it for programmes and data storage. I eventually added a disk drive to the setup. One day there was a fierce thunderstorm and the telephone line to our house was struck by lightning. This destroyed our telephone, the modem, and the central processor of the computer. My house insurance company had never had such an exotic claim before and settled it. The only other claim we ever made was for a surplice which the washing machine decided to scorch when the drying function went a bit wrong.

At Church House, one of the pleasant tasks was helping radio or television programme researchers to find competent church people who could contribute to their programmes. One day I was rung up by a researcher who asked me if I could help with some contacts who could contribute to a documentary to be made about suffering. I gave her some names and numbers and asked her if she was going to include any Jews among her contributors. She said no and seemed genuinely puzzled at the question. I told her that the Jewish community knew more about suffering than many others and gave her some suggestions for leads to follow. She eventually rang off with a new perspective for her programme.

One day I was rung up by Paul Brown, deputy chief executive of the Radio Authority. Did I know of a cricketing grace which could be used at a lunch to honour cricket commentator Brian Johnstone's eightieth birthday? I went down to the Church House bookshop but found nothing that even came close to cricket. I wrote a cricketing grace and faxed it through. Paul rang the next day to say it was the first time he had known a grace attract a round of applause. Not long after this, he rang again to ask if I could write a radio grace for a meal at the Radio Academy. I wrote a broadcasting grace and sent it to him. The next morning when I clocked in at Church House Reception, I found that a bottle of Lanson Black Label champagne had been left for me.

The most challenging grace I was asked to write was for a luncheon at which fifty holders of the Victoria Cross would be present during the Royal Tournament at Earl's Court. I took some time to write this and faxed it to the organisers. They were pleased with it and asked me if I would like two tickets for the Royal Tournament. I cheekily declined and asked for two tickets to the Boat Show instead.

Another challenge was arranging for a documentary video to be made about the Church of England. My heart sank a bit at the prospect as before I left St Albans Diocese there was a madcap idea about a video programme about the diocese which neither the education adviser Jean Stilwell nor I had been told was to be made. I think Jean found out about it by chance. It was a nightmare, as no-one had really thought about the point or purpose of such a thing. It's a story probably best left untold.

Back at Church House I wrote a brief for the programme which was approved and sent out to thirteen possible programme makers for them to consider and make a costed estimate and treatment. Someone was kind enough to say it was the best brief he had ever seen. I wanted the video to work introducing new church members, baptism courses, for established church members to see what other dioceses were doing to inform their ideas about ministry and mission. I saw this being achieved by storytelling from different areas of the Church in England. The best bid at around £30,000 for a half-hour video came from Claire

Walmsley, a distinguished producer and journalist with over twenty years' experience with the BBC. She had formed a media production company called Box Clever. Her treatment won the contract, and the film was everything we had wanted. The then-presenter of the Radio 4 *Today* programme, Brian Redhead, agreed to voice the programme, I think without fee.

We offered it to the parish clergy for the small sum of £10, and Denise took the orders and saw that the 3,000 or so VHS copies were sent to the customers. We only had one priest who complained that it was not what he wanted and please could he have his money back. Helpful to a fault, we said no.

Steve Jenkins' desk and mine were back to back so we faced each other from behind our computers. One year, Steve told me about The Children's Society Family Fun Day, and we decided that we should do something to raise money from Church House, the Church Commissioners on Millbank, and from the Archbishop's staff across the Thames in Lambeth Palace. I imagine we must have got someone's permission for this tiny distraction from the work of the Communications Unit. Perhaps we forgot to ask.

I had once been one end of a pantomime horse at a fundraising fete while a member of All Saints Church in Upper Norwood in the 1960s. I discovered that someone working for the Board of Social Responsibility had access to a pantomime horse suit so I asked if we might borrow it for this event. They not only said yes but found a short secretary to inhabit the back end of the horse costume.

Almost at the last minute of the day before this adventure I became anxious about our safety while trotting on London's busy roads, especially as our route would take us through two busy roundabouts either side of the River Thames. I rang the Press Officer at Scotland Yard and asked whether it would be possible to borrow a mounted police person to keep us safe. 'Leave it with me, and I'll phone you back,' was the response. Sure enough, I was later rung to be told that at 10 a.m. the next day a mounted police officer would meet us at the north door of Church House in Great Smith Street. 'Just one thing, sir,' he said, 'our police horses are trained to deal with civil disorder, traffic, and riots. There is nothing in their training that features pantomime horses, so make no sudden moves.' I thanked him and went home.

The next day dawned sunny and bright and we got into the horse suit and made our way to the north door with one or two colleagues who would collect the money for us. Outside, a lovely policewoman waited mounted on a very splendid police horse. We were careful not to do anything untoward and we set off for Lambeth Palace. I was glad I had secured an escort as all the roads were busy and the police escort shielded us from harm. When we got to Horseferry Road, we passed a flower stall and I suggested that we buy some flowers for the Archbishop's wife, Mrs Carey. We arrived at Lambeth Palace, perhaps the first and maybe only pantomime horse to gain admission on official business, though I suspect a few donkeys may have passed that way.

In the courtyard in front of the Palace, the Archbishop was waiting to greet us, so we knelt the horse in front of him. He said, 'I don't know whether to confirm you or ordain you. Maybe I'll just bless you.' This he did and we toured the palace and the offices collecting for The Children's Society.

We made our way back to Church House via the offices of the Church Commissioners on Millbank. We were generally generously received, except for one accountant's office. We opened the door and looked in and almost before we had time to say who we were and what we were doing, the occupant said, 'Go away.' So, we did.

After Millbank we returned to Church House and collected on all the different floors. One office stood out. It was the office of the education officer for the Church of England, on, I think, the fourth floor. A door opened and we looked in. The chief education officer was in the middle of an employment interview and had just got to the point in the process where he said to the applicant, 'Is there anything

As the front end of the pantomime horse with police escort!

you would like to ask us?' In we trotted. I would love to know how the interview continued.

When we finished, we had collected around £400 for The Children's Society. Freed from the horse suit after some three hours or more, I was ready to curl up and sleep. I stretched out on the office floor and Drina Barnden brought me a glass of whisky. From where, I had no idea, and wasn't minded to ask. It was most welcome and restorative.

The following year we wondered what to do on the Family Fun Day. We came up with the idea of storming Lambeth Palace dressed as a bunch of scary pirates. The Children's Society arranged for about five of us to be kitted out by a noted firm of theatrical costumiers and wigmakers. We certainly looked the business as we ran with our cutlasses across Parliament Square. Looking back, I am surprised we were not arrested. I had arranged for the local Royal Navy Volunteer Reserve to transport us across the Thames from Westminster to Lambeth Pier.

When we arrived at Lambeth Palace, there was Archbishop George Carey all ready to be held at cutlass point until he handed over a cheque for the charity. We returned via the Church Commissioners and Church House offices with a considerable haul for the Society. We wondered what on earth we might do next. It wasn't long before I found out.

In January 1993 there was to be a meeting of the Primates of the Anglican Communion and the Anglican Consultative Council in South Africa and I was chosen to join the ten-person communications team. Given that my experience and training had been in broadcasting, it was not a great surprise to learn that I would be the second photographer working with the Venerable Lynn Ross from Canada and James Thrall from the United States. The conference was to meet at The University of the Western Cape, Cape Town. Our hosts for the two weeks were Archbishop Desmond Tutu and the Church of the Province of South Africa.

We flew from London, changing planes in Holland, and arrived quite weary in Cape Town. Within two hours of arrival on the university campus, where there were delightful signs put up directing visitors to the Primates' meeting, we were in our first briefing meeting on an upper floor in one of the university blocks. Our chaplain to the communications team led by James Rosenthal of the Anglican Consultative Council, was Archbishop of Armagh Robin Eames.

It was very hot and as I sat at the back in this classroom, a butterfly flew in through a window to my left, fluttered across the room and left through a window to my right. I found myself standing on the desk and running after the butterfly while shouting, 'it's an omen, an omen' and making as if to climb out of the window to follow wherever the butterfly led. I hope and pray this helped to ease some of the tiredness and tension that attends the first meeting of a new team in unfamiliar circumstances.

Came the day of a historic meeting between Archbishop George Carey; Archbishop Desmond Tutu; the Anglican Church's first official observer at the United Nations, Sir Paul Reeves; and South Africa's State President Willem de Klerk. I went along as second photographer and took whatever pictures seemed promising and appropriate. It was as well I did as when we returned to the university campus, we discovered that there had been a problem with the other photographer's camera and my pictures were the only photographic record of the meeting.

Interestingly one innovation at this conference was that except for working groups, delegates sat in permanent groups around round tables.

One of the visits I covered with my camera was a visit to one of the townships. I lurked waiting for the photo to compose itself, and it did. A trio of archbishops in purple strode away on litter-covered ground from the extraordinary chaos of the township while the mountains stood dark in the background. Whoever put together the final report of this conference 'A Transforming Vision, suffering and glory in God's world', put this picture on the back of the book. Leafing through some papers I found an Award of Excellence for special achievement in Church Communications 'presented to Anglican World for Photography – Entire issue – Magazine: Agency level – Patrick Forbes, photographer.' I had either never noticed receiving this or had completely forgotten about it.

This visit to South Africa was an eye-opener. I had called at Cape Town and Durban when I was barely twenty years old and had grown to learn more and more about the criminal policy of apartheid. Here I was some thirty-three years later, on the edge of the end of apartheid, taking photographs showing both hope and distress.

I was able to arrange a telephone interview with Barry Amis back at BBC Radio Bedfordshire from the conference Eucharist in the Good Hope Centre, leaving my photographer hat on one side for the few minutes needed. Some ten thousand people turned out for the service led by Archbishop Desmond Tutu with the sermon from Archbishop George Carey, the largest congregation he had ever addressed. The service lasted almost three hours.

One of my more bizarre tasks after lunch one day was to photograph all the archbishops present, in order to bring up to date the photographic records of the Anglican Consultative Council. One by one they filed past me while I took their pictures.

It was an interesting experience, seeing more of the breadth of membership and thought of the Anglican Communion, some 80 million strong in membership at the time. I would not have missed it. One of the highlights was the visit to the conference of the future State President of South Africa, Nelson Mandela.

Later in 1993 I heard that The Children's Society and *The Daily Mail* and Eurotunnel were arranging for around 117 people to walk through the Channel Tunnel shortly before it opened early in 1994. The event on Saturday, 12 February, was to mark the seven years since the signing of the treaty between England and France agreeing to the tunnel's construction. Half the walkers would raise money for The Children's Society and half would walk for other charities. I rang Terry Warburton, the Walk's project director, and said that I thought someone from the Church of England's headquarters should be walking through the tunnel. Were there any places left? 'A few, how much are you going to raise for us?' Typically, I had no idea what the going rate was. I admitted as much and was told that unless I could raise over £10,000, I should forget the whole idea. I said I would do it, put the phone down, and then thought, 'What on earth have I just done?'

What I had just done was to say that I would walk thirty-one miles through the Channel Tunnel and that I would raise over £10,000 in sponsorship for The Children's Society. Was I mad? I was nearing the age of fifty-five. I liked walking but never did any serious distance walking. In fact, I had walked from Wells to Yeovil a couple of times in 1967–1968 and walked thirty-one miles for Christian Aid while at Abbey Wood and Thamesmead. That walk had nearly crippled me, I remembered, having forgotten all about it until that precise moment.

In no time at all I began to get letters from the Society saying scary things like, 'By now you should have walked ten miles, fifteen miles, twenty, thirty miles.' I started to walk from St Pancras Station to Church House most weekday mornings. I joined a ten-mile walk along the banks of the Grand Union Canal. Then I walked almost fifteen miles to St Albans from Lilley on a rainy Saturday morning. I made the mistake of stopping for a swift half pint of beer in Sandridge, not quite at St Albans. As I sat my muscles started to tighten and I nearly couldn't stand by the time I met Annette and her mother at The Peacock Inn at the top of Holywell Hill, St Albans. So, fifteen miles was the furthest I walked in training before the walk itself.

I have mentioned clergy and radio nightmares before. Now the nightmares concerned not being fit enough and being carried out of the tunnel on a stretcher in considerable disgrace. We were told that if any of the walkers got fifteen minutes behind the main body of walkers, they would be taken off the walk. More worrying still were the nightmares around the matter of raising the £10,000 I had promised. As usual Denise Woodford turned up trumps in overseeing the mechanics of handling the money while I fretted at collecting it, prising it out of people's accounts. I wrote to all the diocesan bishops, promising that if they came up with some sponsorship, I would never write to them again. Of those who replied, some said they had no money which I found a little hard to believe. I wrote to my old school who didn't even reply. I asked my former theological college fellow student Paul Bates if Westminster Abbey, on whose staff he was, might contribute. He doubted he would succeed as the Abbey, itself a charity, needed all the money it could find. Paul later got in touch to say that I had made Abbey history by being awarded a £500 contribution and that the story of the donation was being added to their archives. I wrote to building societies, to everyone I could think of and a few I couldn't. Slowly, very slowly the money came in, and before the actual walk, Denise had banked some hundred or so pounds over the £10,000 I had promised to raise.

I asked BBC Bedfordshire if they would like me to make a programme about the event and, bless them, they said yes. This turned out to be a lifesaver and made up for the fact that by the day of the walk my training had not included a walk of thirty-one miles, but rather half that distance.

I started recording pieces for the programme, an interview with the manager of the shoe shop in Hitchin who sold me the trainers I used for training and the walk itself. I spoke to the Society about the walk and its planning. I still have the shoes.

The day before the walk, we were taken across to France and put up in a hotel where we had a delicious dinner while being urged not to drink too much. For once free of nightmares, and possibly anaesthetised by delicious wine, I slept like a top. We had breakfast and were taken to the tunnel mouth at Coquelles where we were sent on our way with a rocket being fired by a *Blue Peter* presenter and a marvellously not-quite-in-tune French town band. I had already interviewed some walkers on the ferry crossing to France, and while we waited at the mouth of the tunnel I talked to Kris Akabusi, some twenty years younger than me, former Olympic athlete and motivational speaker.

Offering to make a radio programme saved the day for me as once we had started walking, the miles flew beneath my feet as I recorded conversations with so many of the walkers. I remember talking to Todd Carty, a member of the cast of *EastEnders*, who was walking for Barnardo's as he had been a Barnardo boy. He had trained by playing football, he told me. I'm not too sure that football was the best training exercise as I heard later that he had come within striking distance of being taken off the walk as his feet were in such a bad way. I spoke to an actress who was learning her lines for a forthcoming part in a play. There was the Bishop of Dover who had worked in our diocese before becoming a bishop. I met a lady in her eighties who wheel-chaired her way through the tunnel. The hours passed and eventually it was lunch time and we stopped briefly to eat food which was provided by the organisers.

When we had walked some nineteen miles or so we reached a great cavern where the railway tracks could cross over. As we approached, we heard Caribbean music being played, and as we emerged into the space, there was a calypso band playing and a good few of the walkers dancing around in a conga. I thought 'How can they be doing that?' In no time at all found that I had joined in. Anything to keep the legs moving. My feet were almost alright but on taking my trainers and socks off, I found some blisters under my toes. A helpful prison officer from Belmarsh Prison, Thamesmead, kindly applied some plasters to relieve the rubbing. There was food and more liquids available here to keep us going for the last twelve miles.

Psychologically it was great good sense for us to be walking towards home from France and not the other way round. I don't think as many would have completed the distance if we had set out from Kent.

When we got to the English entrance to the tunnel, we were early for our appearance on some live television show, so we had to wait around in the cold night air wrapped up in foil to ward off hypothermia. Annette had arrived to watch us finish the walk, and she and David Matthiae, now a vicar in Kent, also waited in the cold for our appearance. We lined up and were presented with some medal or other to commemorate the walk. Richard Branson was there in person and I received a medal and some other goodies to show I had completed the walk. Months later, Annette and I found that my name had been inscribed in a list of the walkers on a stainless-steel commemorative plaque when we took the car on a train through the tunnel to France, a journey timed at around half an hour instead of the twelve to thirteen hours it took us to walk those thirty-one miles.

The next morning, I had to get up early to be at BBC Radio Kent at Sun Pier in Chatham to do a down-the-line piece into BBC Radio 2's *Good Morning Sunday* programme hosted by Don MacLean. I tried to get out of bed and fell on the floor as my legs didn't feel like working after the walk the day before. Somehow, I managed to get washed, shaved, and dressed in time for David to take me into Chatham. There was a moment when I thought I wouldn't be let into the radio station. There aren't too many people about at that time on a Sunday morning, as I should have remembered.

At some point in the previous year, I had had my work assessed, something that as far as I knew had never happened to me before. I remember little if anything of the report except that it said something like, 'If he has a fault it is a tendency to over-commitment.' Maybe that was a back-handed reference to my coming in unpaid to read through all the daily papers.

My four-year contract would expire in 1995 and I was encouraged by management to apply for it to be renewed. Following what I thought was a very positive assessment of my work to date, I applied and was turned down flat. I really could not get to the bottom of why this should be. I wrote to the Secretary General, Philip Mawer, who had been cabinet secretary in Mrs Thatcher's government before coming to lead the work at Church House. His reply made no sense to me, so there I was staring at the end of my time at Church House. I had certainly not run out of ideas. Would I ever? There was plenty of work to do, but it had been decided somewhere that I should not be allowed to continue despite my glowing assessment. Perhaps I shouldn't have been half a pantomime horse, or a pirate, or a Channel Tunnel walker, but I am glad that I was. One of the possible reasons for the contract not being renewed was that there was a new director of communications to be appointed and someone thought he should be free to choose and appoint his team members. This clearly did not apply to the lay members of the team.

I took it very badly. I was not convinced of any of the reasoning behind the refusal to renew the contract. I was due to write some 'Pauses for Thought' for BBC Radio 2 and I remember writing all six of them one Sunday morning before lunch at home in Lilley. They were all around the value of friendship. That was useful therapy. Chris and Christina Rees were living not far away from us in Barley and they invited us for a weekend to cheer us up. That helped too.

Bishop John Taylor had moved on from being chairman of the Church of England Committee for Communications. His successor kindly wrote and asked if I wanted to talk about my situation. I courteously declined as since his appointment we had not seen him in the unit once. We had caught sight of him walking past the office door, but I don't remember him ever coming to meet us.

There I was out of a job and with a £9,000-a-year mortgage to pay for the house which we had bought from St Albans Diocese. I discovered a helpful book of advice for the almost unemployed called *What Colour Is Your Parachute?* One of its suggestions was to tell everyone without exception that you were looking for a job. I followed this advice as best I could. Before my contract expired, Gillian Ennis rang from the Missions to Seamen. She and I had met, and I had been asked for some advice to do with publicity for the Society which I had bumped into at the end of the 1950s when I was a radio officer. I dealt with the matter in hand and asked her if she had any jobs on offer. Curious coincidence, the Missions had just advertised, interviewed, and appointed its first ever press officer. The successful candidate had told his employer, a major daily newspaper who had offered him a significant pay rise and asked him to stay. Was I interested? Is the Pope a Catholic, do bears . . . in the woods? I was keen and asked about the salary. Alas, it was almost exactly £9,000 less than I was being paid at Church House. On the other hand, no parish I could imagine would want someone as old as me to work for them. So, I agreed to go to The Missions to Seamen.

Leaving Church House was a wrench. I was very happy there and on good days I thought we did some good and useful work. Perhaps that was the problem with my employers. The ghostly voice of Jim Thompson could be heard saying, 'Just one idea a year, Patrick.'

Church House was quite unlike any other part of the church I had encountered. I had seen some sort of administrative apparatus in St Albans. I concluded that although I was the communications officer, I wasn't convinced that the Church was that committed to communications. I remember the editor of the Hemel Hempstead *Post Echo* addressing some fellow clergy at a Communications Day workshop I organised. 'You clergy ring me up and ask me to help you with a church event. We give you publicity, balloons, posters, and much more. And then we don't hear from you until the fete in the following year.' Indeed, when leaving the diocese's employment I thought it would be a kindness if I threw out all the files relating to my time there, as a spur for my successor to try some different approach not prejudiced by what I had attempted, so I did. Church House is unique, hosting as it does the Church's national civil service. If I were to ask a representative number of its workers what it was all for, I imagine I would hear any number of answers. A forensic examination of the place, the people, and the work would reveal any number of elephants in full view in so many of those offices.

CHAPTER 16

Seafarers again

The Missions to Seamen, founded in 1856, is in my view one of the best of the Anglican Church's missionary societies. Through its network of over 200 seafarers' centres it meets the needs of seafarers around the world, needs which are becoming more demanding as ships get bigger and faster and crews become smaller and more stressed. One of the heroes at the Mission was the justice secretary, Canon Ken Peters, who worked tirelessly through official and unofficial channels to improve the seafarers' lot around the world. For a large part of his time when I was there, he was battling against cancer as well as doing vital work for the Mission.

A story which illustrates the hazards of seagoing is that of the cargo ship *Caribe 1* which was heading down channel en route to a port in Colombia when the captain noticed that Newhaven was staying obstinately abeam of the ship, despite the engine pushing as hard as it could against the tide. He requested a pilot come out to the ship and take it into port. The pilot ashore looked at the ship through his binoculars and at first was not keen. He boarded the ship, steered her safely into Newhaven, and ensured that she was moored inside a swing bridge. I suspect that he could see that all was far from well.

The ship, built in Germany, had been bought by its Colombian owner who had sent just three seafarers to sail it and its bulk cargo to Colombia. The first we knew about it was as a result of the three Spanish-speaking Colombian mariners arriving for Evensong at the parish church in Newhaven, whose priest was an honorary Missions to Seamen chaplain. The seafarers managed to explain their plight. They had little money, not enough food to eat on board, and their ship was to be inspected by the Maritime and Coastguard Agency. I was asked to go and take photographs of the ship's condition.

It was in a shocking state. All the emergency notices and signs were in German, which the Colombians could neither read nor speak. The hull was pitted with rust. Access to the engine room from the deck was via a door that was supposed to be watertight but wasn't; seawater penetrated through the seals and fell onto the emergency generators situated below the door.

The ship was inspected, the cargo was found to be unsafely stowed, there was not the requisite number of seafarers to take the ship safely across the Atlantic, and repairs would have to be carried out, paid for, and adequate water and provisions put aboard to last until the Canary Islands where the ship was to be inspected again before being allowed to proceed across the Atlantic to Colombia. Meanwhile the sailors were looked after by the Anglican Church in Newhaven.

This was not the worst case of criminal neglect handled by the Mission, which eventually changed its name to Mission to Seafarers to take account of the women employed at sea. One estimate I heard was that, worldwide, some 10 per cent of shipowners are believed to be crooks. Ships and seafarers are worked to death and then abandoned by the owners with wages unpaid, and no food on board. The Mission, through its chaplains, seafarers' centres, and contacts with lawyers, does all it can for the welfare of the mariners and their families. Ships are visited, seafarers of all nationalities and faiths made welcome, visited in prison or hospital, and contacts made with families at home across the world.

My office in the Mission to Seafarers was on the third floor of the Wren Church of St Michael Paternoster Royal, in College Hill near Cannon Street station. There was no natural light in the office, and there was no lift. When I joined the Mission in 1995 the absence of a lift was no problem. I could easily run up the stairs to the office.

I wrote press releases, drafted the speech of the Mission's president, Her Royal Highness the Princess Royal, for the annual meeting of the society. I always tried to put something in her speech which would catch the eyes of journalists, but her press office generally weeded out such content. I was introduced to the mysteries of PageMaker, the Adobe publication software, and wrote a regular contribution to the Mission's newspaper for seafarers, *The Sea*. I helped with the writing, pictures, and layout of the Mission's regular publication for supporters, *Flying Angel News*.

I once had to go and talk about communications to a meeting of supporters in Surrey. I was due to speak at 11 a.m., after coffee. It was only some fifty-six miles from Lilley but as the journey meant using the M25 motorway around London, I left at 6.30 in the morning. Everything went well for a while, but I was soon caught up in a three-hour traffic jam on the motorway. Minutes and hours passed. I thought of doing a John Cleese in *Fawlty Towers* and getting out of the car and hitting it with a stick. Then I saw the Mission to Seafarers sticker in the rear window and thought better of the idea. Eventually I was able to leave the motorway and make my way across country via Windsor. This being before I had a mobile phone, I found a phone box where the phone had not been vandalised and rang the regional director's mobile to say I was on my way and should be there at some point, but he might want to rearrange the programme. I arrived at the conference venue and walked in to hear the regional director say, 'At this point we had hoped to bring you Patrick Forbes from Head Office. . . .' I later found that an articulated lorry had jack-knifed on the motorway, losing its load of Yorkshire puddings as it did so.

Another close shave occurred when I joined a brand-new coastal tanker in Aberdeen in order to take some up-to-date colour pictures of life at sea for the Mission. The Everard ship, the *Asperity*, was much the same size as the 4,000-ton *Sugar Importer* but instead of a crew of thirty-two, there were just seven or eight seafarers on board. We set off making port calls down the east coast until we arrived off Ipswich in foul weather on a Saturday. I explained to the captain that I needed to disembark that day as I had agreed to baptise the child of a friend in Berkshire on the following afternoon. The captain said he couldn't help as he was not licensed to take the ship into Ipswich and we would have to wait for a pilot to take us in. He rang the port authorities, explained the situation, and they said on this occasion they would waive the rules to allow him to take the ship in and dock so I could get off and away. The crew were delighted that they would be able to get a good night's sleep safely alongside, rather than being pounded by wind and waves at sea. I got some very good pictures during heavy weather, a seafarer being detailed to keep an eye on me while photographing on deck, even though I was secured to the ship by a lifeline while wearing heavy-weather gear and a life jacket.

The Mission usually had a stand at the annual International Boat Show. One year I was in the middle of a series of six 'Pause for Thought' episodes for Radio 2. On the day I was writing one of these, there was a news story about a Shell tanker which had been attacked while berthed in a South American port. Armed villains had boarded the ship, and a woman deck officer had bravely shielded a cadet from them. I wrote the 'Pause for Thought' around this story and went to the BBC to deliver it. After the broadcast I travelled to the Boat Show as I was on the rota for manning the Mission stand. As I arrived, the Princess Royal was talking to our London regional director. She was telling him she was listening to Terry Wogan's breakfast show earlier and there was this story about the tanker and the brave woman deck officer. She wondered who had written and presented this. The regional director saw me arrive and told Princess Anne and she turned round. We had met before, but I don't think she had connected me with 'Pause for Thought.'

Every year at Royal Ascot there is a charity race day. In 1996 the Mission to Seafarers was invited to take part with an eight-legged pantomime horse. The race, over a very short course, was called The Fall-Down Stakes. I fear that we came sixth out of six but it was great fun, and we were introduced to Prince Michael of Kent after the race. In the run-up to the race, we had some pictures taken of the horse with Terry Wogan.

At some point in my time there was the suggestion of a promotional video to be made about the work of the Mission. Fortunately, a researcher rang up one day to say she was involved in making a series of documentaries for, I think, Channel Five. The theme was to do with sacred places. She asked if we had any old buildings. I said probably not as the Society was founded as recently as the nineteenth century. However, I said, there was a splendid place she should investigate. It was a new seafarer's

Terry Wogan and our pantomime horse

centre set among petrochemical installations on the north of the River Tees. We had a remarkable chaplain there, Ken Cornforth, who I was sure would be a very competent contributor with a host of stories to tell.

Luckily, she investigated it and the seafarers' centre and the Mission featured throughout one of the programmes. Knowing we were looking for a promotional video, I negotiated with Channel Five that we could be supplied with a Betamax broadcast-quality copy of the programme from which we could make as many VHS copies as we liked absolutely free provided that we didn't charge anyone for watching it.

This was ideal as it meant we had a professionally made programme we could show to members and supporters of the Mission at no cost to the society. I remember one of the stories that Ken Cornforth told me. He went on board ship and met a seafarer who gave all the signs of mental breakdown. He had been at sea for months and was at the end of his rope. Ken took him ashore, bundled him into his car, and drove him away from the docks out into the country. He parked next to a field and took the seafarer into the field where he just sat down and cried, surrounded by grass and trees for the first time he could remember in a long time. With his tears, all his pent-up tension flowed out and evaporated. He returned to his ship heartened and restored. I suspect that all the Mission's chaplains and lay ship visitors could tell a stack of similar stories.

I never quite 'swallowed the anchor,' something you're supposed to do when coming ashore to do some land-based job. The sea draws me back. It is a powerful metaphor for life. Looking back, I see so much in my life to do with journeying, travelling. My time at sea, driving thousands of miles for Robophone, and the programme with Chiltern which we called *Travelling*, then *Travellers' Tales* with Premier Christian Radio. I find the sea inspirational, terrifying in its mood changes, and the speed of those changes from calm to raging fury.

Seagoing has mattered to me. It matters still. I don't claim to have learned enough to feel entirely safe at sea. If anyone so claims, then they are either a liar or a fool of the worst kind. The sea is always there, plotting to kill the careless, the unsuspecting, or the downright unlucky. It is no surprise to me that some of the earliest followers of Jesus were down-to-earth fishermen. Seafarers know the hazards of their trade, they know that if they don't pull together, if they don't watch out for each other, they will be individually picked off by that misleadingly beautiful ocean.

I believe one of the best Christian metaphors is that of the journey, the voyage, the pilgrimage, new sights, new sounds every day, course steered, distance gained, space to reflect on life, love, the universe, God, time to think, consider maybe even believe.

CHAPTER 17

Retirement – what retirement?

In my last eighteen months at the Mission, I had found climbing the stairs more and more of a challenge. Eventually it got so bad that I applied to the Church of England Pensions Board about the possibility of early retirement on the grounds of ill health. They said I should get thoroughly checked over by a doctor, they would send me the paperwork, and, by the way, 'You don't have to die to be allowed to retire early on the grounds of ill health.' That was a relief to know. By now we had moved from Lilley to the village of Hinxworth, just a few hundred yards from the border between North Hertfordshire and Mid Bedfordshire. Annette's parents had both died, and the money from selling her mother's flat in Hitchin together with what we had made from the sale of the house in Lilley enabled us to buy a former council-built old people's bungalow which had been extended to the side and to the rear, and tentatively into the roof space.

We had spent six dispiriting months looking for somewhere else to live, exploring hovels, wrecks, and ruins across Hertfordshire and Cambridgeshire. One Saturday morning we were on our way to look at six more prospects when we decided to look at an estate agent's window in Ashwell. There was a picture of a bungalow in Hinxworth, on sale for £110,000 a price we could just afford. We rushed into the shop and asked if we could view the house that day. No, we were told, but tomorrow was possible. So, after church the following day, we came to Hinxworth to look at the house. We knew within ten minutes it was just what we wanted. We investigated the roof space and saw that we could put a bedroom and a bathroom up there. We said that if they took it off the market, we would seal

Home in Hinxworth

the deal there and then at the price they were asking. The sellers did not want to move but the husband had been offered a seat on the board of the company who employed him if he would move with the firm to somewhere in the west country. We were most fortunate, we were told, as a fireman based at Watford had bought it the previous week but, on telling of his future change of address, he had been told that he couldn't live in Hinxworth and be based at Watford. His loss was our gain.

Back to the early retirement question. I went to the surgery in Ashwell and was given a thorough going-over which revealed no obvious cause. 'We're going to have to say stress and exhaustion,' said the doctor. The papers were sent off to the Pensions Board and in no time at all I received word that my early retirement on the grounds of ill health had been approved, my pension would be this amount, here was the lump sum, and be sure to enjoy your retirement.

I was conscience stricken for around ten seconds until I remembered the mountains of work at Thamesmead, two parishes and a sort of full-time job for St Albans. Maybe I had done the required thirty-seven years' work in thirty-two years. I stopped fretting and left the Mission to Seafarers. I had been happy there, had done a lot of writing and photography, and learned about laying out publications, and with any luck done some useful work on behalf of seafarers who were becoming more invisible and more preyed upon by the day.

In 1999 my brother Mike wrote to me and said that he had been diagnosed as having haemochromatosis, a genetic disorder in which the body fails to metabolise iron which over time builds up in joints and vital organs and if undiagnosed can result in liver or heart failure. I should make sure that both I and our son Stephen were checked out to see if we had inherited the defective genes.

I went to the surgery, asked for the test, had it done, and I did indeed have the disorder. I was referred to Addenbrooke's Hospital in Cambridge. The treatment for the condition is simple and straightforward. One estimate was that I had about thirteen times the acceptable level of ferritin in my system. Mike's level was much higher. For a year I went every fortnight to Addenbrooke's where a unit of blood was taken from me. Over time this removal of blood lowers the level of ferritin to a less harmful figure. For some months I was able to continue being a blood donor but then some bureaucratic mix-up put a stop to that. Eventually I learned that my blood was of some use to the hospital department studying malaria. Mosquitoes were imported from Africa and my iron rich blood was being used to keep the little blighters alive. Given my antipathy towards mosquitoes and their obvious liking for me and my blood, maybe there is some justice here.

A charity, the Haemochromatosis Society, was formed by the widow of a man who died of the disease before it was diagnosed. The charity aims to encourage research into the condition and educate both the medical profession and the general public to its existence, symptoms, and treatment. I believe that the condition is the second most widespread genetic disorder after colour blindness in the United

Kingdom. Given that the treatment is now routine, the greatest need is for the symptoms to be recognised.

It seems that the disorder is most prevalent wherever the Vikings have been – Scandinavia; the east and west coasts of the United Kingdom; Ireland; Brittany, Spain, and Portugal; and Australia, though I don't think the Vikings were there.

Should I have cancelled my retirement once the haemochromatosis had been diagnosed and treated? I don't think so. Once we had moved to Hinxworth, we found there was a vacancy in the United Benefice of Ashwell, Hinxworth and Newnham. I immediately dived in to help with taking services at St Nicholas Church in this village, and in Ashwell or Newnham as required. Hinxworth has a population of around 250 to 300. There once was a shop and a school. Now there is a pub, a village hall, and the present church built in 1322. One of the stories told me when we moved to Hinxworth was that the Diocese of St Albans had appointed a house for duty priest James Laing, confident that the church would close and be made redundant. They were probably disappointed. James Laing was a huge hit with the villagers and the church obstinately remained open.

I was appalled by this story of diocesan mischief and I checked it out years after Bishop John Taylor retired and moved to Madingley near Cambridge. I went to see the bishop to record a programme for Premier Christian Radio. Before starting the recording, I asked if the story was true and he said it was.

Vacancies or interregna are both good and bad, symptomatic of much of the mess that disfigures the Church of England. The convention seems to be that clergy give three months' notice of their intention to move or retire. A diocese sometimes insists on being asked if the post may be advertised and generally rules that no advertisement may be placed until the priest has physically left the parish, lest he or she change their mind and want to stay. So inevitably there are six months without a priest being in post. Meanwhile parishes can be without a priest for months or years depending on how fast or slowly the church

St Nicholas, Hinxworth

authorities move. While there is no priest, the parish is only required to pay a percentage of its parish share for the training, appointment, and housing of a priest – a percentage, I am told, that can be as high as 80 or 95 per cent. Meanwhile the churchwardens are responsible for seeing that the life of the parish with its services and meetings continues with as little sign as possible that there is no priest.

When a priest is put into a parish by a bishop, the bishop hands the cure of souls to the priest, saying that the responsibility is both his and the priest's. There aren't enough bishops to handle the cure of souls in vacant parishes at any one time, so it falls to Readers and retired clergy to do what they can. Some months ago, there were twenty-two vacancies in this part of the diocese. There is never a surplus of ordained clergy to cope with vacancies, so parishes must make do.

It is possible to see a vacancy as both a curse and a blessing, and I have seen both. Parishes can mourn or celebrate the departure of a priest but there are practical things to be done in the absence of a priest. People, adults and children need to be baptised, weddings taken, the sick visited, the dead buried. A healthy organisation responsible for caring for people and which delights in affirming that no-one in England is beyond the care of the nationwide network of parishes, would cater for the inevitable occurrence of vacancies either by increasing the number of clergy available to cover them, or by speeding up the process of advertising posts and appointing clergy to parishes.

I believe and hope that the Methodist Church does things better. It used to be the case, I am told, that to try and hire a removal firm during August would be a wasted effort as all Methodist ministers moved to new posts during that month, evidence of a lack of madness in Methodism, a kind of Methodist ministerial excuse-me!

Since we have been here in Hinxworth there have been four vacancies, the last one considerably complicated by debates about the selling of the Georgian rectory in Ashwell, in appearance a fine building, but impossible to heat. One priest said that it cost him some £25 a day to keep just a small part of the house comfortable to live in. It was said that Ashwell rectory's upkeep swallowed up most of Hertfordshire's parsonage maintenance budget. There were debates within the parish and between the parish and the diocese before it was decided to sell the rectory and buy or build a modern affordable replacement. The heat generated by the debates could probably have warmed the rectory for some months. 'Why doesn't the priest wrap up more warmly, or just live in one room' was the level at which some points were made.

Every parish is required to draw up an assessment of the state of the parish and some sort of identity profile of the priest it would like appointed. To this end, there are meetings where churchwardens from the parishes within a benefice meet and try to agree on the qualities of the person they would like to see as priest.

I wrote that vacancies can be both good and bad. They can be good when the lack of a parish priest leads to a burst of creativity and projects are planned and executed before another priest comes on the scene. It matters too that congregations learn that they may very well be more resourceful than they imagined. All kinds of ideas can be suggested, trialled, and if they work become part of the fabric of the place before the new priest appears. Change during vacancy is officially frowned upon, it is fair to say.

Nonetheless something needs to be done about vacancies. Caring organisations, among which the Church of England might believe itself to be, would not allow a situation to exist when the primary carer simply isn't there for maybe one or two years or more. A local vacancy took three years to fill.

In October 2001, I inaugurated my second *Village Voice* project. The first, serving Offley, Lilley, Mangrove, Cockernhoe, and Tea Green, is thriving. Its latest edition, twenty pages long, number 431, has just arrived.

The first edition of *Village Voice* for Caldecote, Edworth, Hinxworth, and Newnham carried on its front page the results of some academic research looking into the prospects for people growing old in Hinxworth. Commissioned by the Community Development Agency for Hertfordshire, it upset at least one villager who later told me that he had not opened the paper since. I replied that I thought that that was his loss. The paper is now on its third editor. I looked after it for some fourteen years, give or take, and it was a blessing to give it up last year, freeing up two to three days a month. It was generously printed by our Roman Catholic churchwarden's civil engineering company. When he retired, a villager from Edworth took it on and it is printed in full colour each month. Like Thamesmead's *Insight*, and Offley's *Village Voice*, it is delivered by volunteers into every home free each month and each edition is what villagers choose to make of it.

While at the Mission to Seafarers, I had become involved on the edge of Premier Christian Radio, voicing the occasional prayer for the day or an interview around Sea Sunday. One day I met the chief executive, Peter Kerridge in the corridor at their offices in Stag Place, Victoria. 'Ah,' he said, 'I think we should get you on air.' I replied that I thought I was. 'No, with your own programme,' he said. 'What would you like to do?' I had never thought for a moment of any such thing.

It was a St George's House Windsor moment. I heard myself say, 'I'd like to record a half-hour interview with people about their journey of faith and at the end ask them who they would like to present with a Bible and why, and promise to do it on their behalf.' He seemed to like the idea, and so the series *Travellers' Tales* was born.

The programmes were recorded and edited to fit a twenty-six-minute slot and broadcast on Sundays on Premier Radio. My time in local radio had taught me that storytelling was an extremely powerful way of communicating ideas. I had absolutely no difficulty in finding people of faith with stories to tell. Although Premier is a Christian Radio station, I was able to record tales with Muslim or Jewish contributors. After the introduction, I always asked the same question: 'What is your earliest recollection of bumping into God?' and off we went. The first programmes were edited, topped, and tailed by a member of Premier's staff. Then I took responsibility for the whole package, arranging the interview, recording and editing and mixing in the music at the front and the end of the programmes.

I had learned the hard physical business of editing tape with one-sided razor blade, Chinagraph pencil, and editing tape. It was such a blessing when I first saw sound editing being carried out on a computer screen. I begged to have a go and in thirty seconds had achieved my first electronic edit. In the beginning I burned the programmes onto compact discs and sent them through the post, which worked well until someone signed for the delivery and then the CD went missing, and the programme had to be rapidly burned onto a fresh disc and rushed to Premier. Every month I wrote to Premier with the details of the Bibles to be sent to people chosen by the contributors I had interviewed. The first programme was recorded with the co-founder of the Christian Resources Exhibition, Gospatric Home. I had attended one of the first such exhibitions at Westminster's Horticultural Hall in the mid-1980s. I wasn't carrying a tape machine but wished I had been when an exhibitor grabbed me and told me of the organisation he worked for. They were stockpiling food and other supplies somewhere in the Holy Land in preparation for the imminent end of the world.

There were occasional hiccoughs with the process. I remember interviewing the head of a Roman Catholic homeless charity in London. He wanted his Bible sent to Prime Minister Margaret Thatcher, but he would like it sent to him first as he wished to underline some passages before sending it to Downing Street. Over the fourteen years I was producing the programme, Bibles were sent around the world, to high and low. I am sure Bibles were sent to President Obama, President Putin, to the head of the world food programme of the United Nations. One contributor wanted his sent to the bosun of a cross-channel ferry who liked to give Bibles to unsuspecting passengers.

Some interviewees, a tiny minority, were worried at the thought of a kind of theological colonialism and asked for their Bibles so they could leave them, as if by accident, on a bus or train where they might be found by God knows who. And that was the point. God could choose who the recipient might be – as if God did not have enough to do!

Before beginning each recording as well as checking microphone levels, I would always tell the interviewee that if he or she wanted something they had said not broadcast, they had only to tell me and I would remove it. Only once or twice was this request ever made and fulfilled. Another important process was the spotting of loud ticking clocks which if ignored would cause problems for the editing process. I always sent a CD copy of the programme to the interviewee once it had been broadcast. I never gave in to requests that they should hear it beforehand.

I recorded most of the programmes where people were at the time, whether that was under the flight path into Heathrow or in Roly Bain's car at a motorway service area off the A34. The most challenging was a programme I made with the singer Maria McKee in her dressing room some few metres from the main stage at Greenbelt Christian Arts Festival on Cheltenham Racecourse. I am surprised anyone heard a word she said.

Sometimes I just happened on likely interviewees. At Greenbelt one year I was on my way to interview the Poet Laureate Andrew Motion. I walked through a book tent and there at one end of the tent was a group of children sitting on the ground, their parents ranged behind them. They were listening to Bible stories told to them by Bob Hartman, a Christian musician and storyteller. But for the wind howling outside you could have heard a pin drop. I waited for a break in the stories and asked him if he would record a *Traveller's Tale* later in the day. He agreed and I went on my way to see Andrew Motion.

In 2005 Annette and I and my sister-in-law Pat went to South Africa for a holiday. I did arrange two interviews before travelling there but, once there, I kept meeting people with stories crying out to be told, we came home with sixteen programmes in the can. One of these was recorded as a result of a visit to the waterside shopping area in Cape Town. On a noticeboard I saw a card mentioning the intriguing words, Original T Bag Designs. I made a note of the phone number, rang them up and discovered a great story. A teacher, Jill Heyes, lived in Suffolk and was married to Charlie who worked in the shipping business. He fell out of work and the only employment he could find was working in Cape Town. They moved to South Africa. Jill was unable to work as a teacher so she was encouraged to start an art group with a bunch of black ladies from the neighbouring township near Hout Bay in the hope that they would begin to produce saleable artwork to begin to lift them out of poverty. 'In no time at all, they were producing unsaleable papier mâché work,' she told me. A friend she had helped some twenty years earlier came out to visit and they were discussing the art group problem over a cup of tea. Her friend pulled the teabag out of her cup and said, 'Can't they do something with this?' Used teabags were collected, emptied of their tea, washed, and ironed, becoming miniature canvases on which the ladies painted traditional African designs from their own heritage and imagination.

In 2007 when we returned for another South African holiday, Original T Bag Designs was producing the most beautiful and original works of art, greeting cards, trays, coasters, jewellery, all fashioned from used tea bags. By then four of the ladies had done so well, they were living in their own new houses, built with access to main services.

Throughout my time with *Travellers' Tales*, I never had any difficulty finding contributors, though I experienced one or two difficulties along the way. I once tried to find a Christian black policewoman in a nightmare complex of flats in an unfamiliar part of North London. This was before I had a car with satnav. I think I was on the point of giving up when I rang her number to find I was quite close, and she told me to keep going as she was cooking a meal for me. There was another contributor who I was completely unable to stop talking and as I drove away, I found that I had fifty-two minutes rather than the thirty minutes I usually achieved. I wickedly thought I would just take out every other word in the editing process. Of course, I didn't, and I hazard a guess that he would not notice where I had made the necessary cuts. One Scotsman interrogated me with questions about whether I had been washed in the blood of the Lamb and all my back history before he would agree to being interviewed. Another contributor suddenly burst into tuneful song when I least expected it.

The five-hundredth *Traveller's Tale* was recorded with the Archbishop of Canterbury Dr Rowan Williams. I asked him how big the contrasts were between being Archbishop of Wales and being the Archbishop of Canterbury. 'Enormous really, working in Wales is working in a small church which is fairly homogeneous. There weren't great extremes of opinion. There were real divisions of course and we had to deal with the women's ordination question like other churches. But essentially, we knew each other quite well. We couldn't quarrel too badly because we were too close to one another. And suddenly you're in a huge global setting where the cultural differences and the theological differences are huge. And that's where I think it's important to hang on to the idea that it is God's church. This isn't an institution that I've got to run . . . or not just that. This is the assembly of people who have been called by God into the fellowship of his Son. Now, the fact that we have all been called into the fellowship of his Son doesn't make us agree or easy to get on with but it does say that the foundation is not our agreement, the foundation is the act of God and therefore there are always grounds for hope.'

I asked the Archbishop how he prayed. 'First and foremost, settle the body, get your body in a position where you don't have to fidget or wriggle. For me that has developed into squatting on my heels with a prayer stool in the mornings. Breathe deeply and get a regular rhythm in your breathing. Let your breath go right down to the pit of your stomach. Then let the words come, just very simple words, "Jesus, have mercy." Let those words float on your breath and keep doing that. Let that become second nature as the period of prayer goes by. Ideas and concerns will come and go. Images will float across your mind. Let them. Not the end of the world but come back to the central activity which is just breathing in, in the Spirit so to speak, and letting the name of Jesus rise out of the centre of your being towards the Father. I have always seen it as a time when we are invited into the life of God the Holy Trinity. There is God the Father inviting us. Here is God the Son giving us his name. Here is God the Holy Spirit supporting us and breathing in us as Spirit. So, when I pray, that's what is going on, it's the life of the Holy Trinity coming alive where I am and where the praying people of God are.'

When I had retired, sort of, our solicitor who was also the Diocesan Registrar, David Cheetham, had advised me solemnly to set up a small, limited liability company, especially as I might want to write something for public consumption. So Forbes Services Ltd. was formed with issued shares in the extravagant sum of £2. I knew nothing about company law, but I suddenly had the nightmare prospect of dealing with Companies House, annual returns, and corporation tax issues. I had never been good at tax. I had been spoilt while at sea when I was taxed at a shilling in the pound and my monthly pay-sheets were a breeze to complete. At one point while at Offley I had fallen four years behind with my annual clergy tax returns, and the authorities began to get cross and put me on emergency tax deductions. It was so silly. With one side of what passes for a brain, I knew that it would take just a morning or afternoon to fill out the wretched clergy tax return, while my other half of the brain was frozen in terror and panic at the thought.

Annette was made of sterner stuff. She reminded me of all the advertisements in the *Church Times* for accountancy help with clergy tax returns. I rang one up and in no time at all, all was in order, sweetness and light returned, and the same company subsequently agreed to look after Forbes Services Ltd's tax business. For them to be able to draw up the company papers, I needed to find a bookkeeper to make sense of all the receipts, invoices, and other stuff. At four o'clock in the morning I remembered that there was a lady round the corner of our road who loved bookkeeping. She readily agreed and for the life of the company she was my stalwart buffer against the slings and arrows of outrageous company financial fortunes and my own personal tax demons.

CHAPTER 18

How soon can you stop making these programmes?

While I was working on *Travellers' Tales*, I also worked with Daphne Hall on some miniseries of shorter programmes. *Round the Clock* was a series of short interviews with essential workers who were Christians. We also made a series called *Prayers, Please*, and a series about coping with bereavement and grief. Daphne had been involved in a project to set up a hospice in Essex. It was great to work with another believer on these programmes.

For some ten years or so I had written and voiced five short 'Thoughts for the Day' for Premier Radio, under the heading of *Forbes on Faith*. One day one of Premier's staff rang up with a question. 'How soon can you stop producing *Forbes on Faith*, Patrick?' I was a bit baffled. I asked why. There was a pause. 'Well, we're tidying up the devotional content of the breakfast show.' This was something new. Tidied up! I said, 'I'll stop in a fortnight's time.' So, after some 2,500 pieces written, recorded, edited, and broadcast, I was tidied up. Fair enough, it was just such a strange way of handling it, I thought. If the roles had been reversed, would I have done it differently, better? I sort of hope so, but I don't know.

While at Church House and the Mission to Seafarers I had been asked to contribute to the Radio 2 'Pause for Thought' slot in the breakfast show. When I first started the programme was presented, from 1986 to 1991, by Derek Jameson, former editor of the *Daily Express*. The format of the 'Pause for Thought' section was being introduced, voicing the script, and then listening to some mildly soothing music before a short conversation with Derek. He used to doodle on a pad

Derek Jameson enjoying his red nose!

during the 'Pause for Thought' and the music that followed, and it was fun trying to read his doodles upside down in case there was a clue to what he might say when the music ended. I never managed the challenge. I found Derek to be a genial presenter and we seemed to get on well. One Red Nose Day he agreed to me taking a picture of him wearing a red nose I had given him.

Bryan Hayes took on the breakfast show after Derek Jameson until Terry Wogan returned to present *Wake Up to Wogan* in 1993. I did several 'Pauses for Thought' and enjoyed many conversations with him. After one script he asked me whether I was keen on sport; he had gained the impression that sport and I did not get on. I answered that I enjoyed the occasional game of croquet using flamingos for mallets and hedgehogs in place of croquet balls, though I was not so explicit, simply mentioning the flamingos and hedgehogs. This light-hearted banter got me into trouble with a listener who wrote to the director general insisting that he take me off air for promoting animal cruelty.

I wrote to her saying that of course this was a reference to Lewis

Carroll's *Alice in Wonderland*, and I was sorry if she did not know about it. I assured her that I would no more display cruelty to animals and that the reference had been in fun. Sometimes it amazes me that anyone ever dares to write or say anything that just might be misunderstood. When I was involved in the clowning workshop at St James' Piccadilly back in 1983, I received an anonymous letter from God, who clearly lived in Oxford for that was where the envelope was postmarked. The letter said that I should hasten to put my affairs in order as the angels would be along shortly to pitch me into the fires of hell for so blaspheming God's house as to clown in it. Oh dear.

Broadcasting live, like the sea, will catch you if your attention slips. One day, some way through a series of six 'Pauses for Thought,' I had been reading the day's script when I was suddenly hurried into the studio and sat down as Terry Wogan said, 'It's 9.15, time for "Pause for Thought" with the Reverend Patrick Forbes.' I looked at my script, it was the one for the week before, left in my pocket with that day's script. There wasn't time to fumble around getting the right one. I knew how it started, knew how it finished, and had a clear idea of the words in between. So I voiced it, unseen. During the next piece of music, I explained to Terry what had happened. He said, 'You wouldn't have guessed, Patrick.' I confessed later to my producer in Manchester who said that apart for a pause perhaps half a second too long, she would not have known. That has never happened again. Nor must it.

When I neared the seven-hundredth *Travellers' Tale*, I wondered whether I should push on, to make it a round thousand. Then I thought about the travelling, the editing, the whole programme business, and decided to stop at 700, almost fourteen years' worth. In the same way that I dread falling asleep in one of my own sermons while preaching it, it would not do to lose interest halfway through an interview. It would seem unfeeling, impolite, downright rude. Premier told me recently that they were thinking of repeating the *Travellers' Tales* series.

I didn't have any regrets other than failing to snare the Archbishop of York and Archbishop Desmond Tutu. It was not for want of trying.

I pursued John Sentamu from the moment he was appointed in 2005. At one point I was told by one of his staff that 'the archbishop doesn't like being interviewed unless he has something to say.' This was about as silly as it gets. All I was asking was for him to spend something over half an hour recording the story of his journey of faith. If he had nothing to say about what, on the surface at least, sounds a fascinating and inspiring pilgrimage, then for nearly the first time, words fail me.

I was within a whisker of interviewing Desmond Tutu in South Africa when the arrangements fell through because a South American government needed him to inaugurate a truth and reconciliation commission in their country. This clearly was a better reason for not recording a *Travellers' Tale* than that offered by the man in York.

It would be fun to write a book drawing on content from those 700 interviews but maybe they are best left in my memory. People have suggested I write a book of thoughts, one for every day of the year, selected from the ten years' worth I wrote and recorded for Premier. Suggestion, I know, is the easy bit. Again and again I have been drawn to storytelling and, even now at this late stage, I wish I was better at it.

One of the best things to happen to me in retirement was a suggestion from our Methodist organist's wife, Dr Pauline Lambourne, a psychiatrist of old age at the Glaxo Day Hospital on the site of the Lister Hospital in Stevenage. One of the groups meeting weekly at the hospital was made up of several patients with early-onset dementia. I am not too sure why Pauline thought my working with them would be a good idea. But I think it turned out to be the case. I joined the 400-strong number of volunteers working with the trust responsible for the Lister Hospital.

I worked with occupational therapists and the dementia group most Thursday afternoons for a couple of hours. From time to time I was given my own session with them. As an example of the daft things we did together, I remember receiving a cheque for twenty pounds which I exchanged for a random collection of ladies' hats from a charity shop in Biggleswade. I took the hats to one of the Thursday sessions.

When the group was ready, I emptied the bag of hats onto the floor in the middle of the group. I asked them to individually pick out a hat, put it on, and do something that someone wearing that hat might do. I had scarcely finished speaking when two ladies rushed to the heap of hats and picked out two wedding hats. Returning to their seats they began accurately reciting words from the marriage service. Another member selected a straw sombrero and, putting it on, danced back to her seat in Mexican tango mode. A new member of the group who didn't want to be there walked slowly to the pile of hats, poked about and chose an army-type camouflage hat, put it on and, maybe in his mind, disappeared from the group while remaining in his place.

I have always liked trying on hats, and indeed anything that might rest on my head. I was excited by this non-verbal exercise in the group and it might have been fun to develop the role-playing process further. Another exercise was with balloons. I divided the group into teams of two and set them to play a sort of mad balloon tennis in which the aim was to keep the balloon in the air with the two teams batting the balloon backwards and forwards across an imaginary net. In no time at all, the service users, clients, patients – whatever was the fashion at the time for calling them – were going at this game with all their energy. By the time we had finished I was worried that one or more of them might have a heart attack.

I had been left alone in the room with this group with no professional member of staff there. I thought this was wrong and wrote to management to say that it was probably unfair or unwise to leave a volunteer with such a group unsupported by a member of staff. This point was taken and accepted.

There can be a problem with volunteers being charged with something beyond their competence, leaving the people with whom the volunteer is working unprotected and at some hazard. People with dementia can sometimes turn violent. One such was a big man, a former weapons inspector, and he had with him a stout stick. One day I walked into one of the rooms where the occupational therapist had been working with him, showing him how much each of several coins was worth. When she finished, he went to scoop up all the coins, which were not his. The therapist tried to get them back from him and I saw a dangerous argument result. I suggested to the therapist that she let the coins go rather than risk some violence. She agreed to do so.

One Christmas I had been given a slot in the annual variety show put on by the staff for the patients. I had some silly songs and comic poems to recite. I was into the first of these which I had remembered from pantomime decades earlier. I danced back and forth singing this silly song, 'Ship ahoy, ship ahoy, I'm a soppy sailor boy. Never ever been to sea, I'm as soppy as I can be' and I turned on my heel just in front of the former weapons inspector who was there with his stick. As I turned, I felt a sharp shooting pain from my right ankle. Not knowing what had caused the pain, I continued in 'the show must go on' mode. I wondered later whether the man had struck me with his stick. After the show I asked for the ankle to be looked at and one of the staff wound a crepe bandage round it, apologised, and said they had taken my cry of pain as being part of the act.

On my way home, I did some shopping in Old Stevenage, drove into Baldock, and had my hair cut. The next morning, I went to see the doctor in Ashwell and he looked at the crepe bandage and said, 'They might as well have wound that round your head for all the good it's doing. You have torn your Achilles tendon and it needs to be plastered. Off you go to A and E at the Lister Hospital in Stevenage.'

When next I went to the early-onset dementia group, the unit manager told me on no account to dance again as she had spent, she said, three days filling in the paperwork needed to explain how a volunteer had had such an accident.

While a volunteer at the Lister, I did a lot of work with the volunteer organiser Janis Hall taking photographs and writing up interviews with some of the volunteers for the annual volunteer magazine. This was fun to do and with any luck promoted the whole volunteering scene at the hospital trust. I came to see how vital the contribution of volunteers is to the running of any hospital.

Among the various activities in the dementia group, I discovered the importance of music. While at the Glaxo Day Hospital I introduced music quizzes. I would select twenty tracks of different kinds of music from pop to classics, music for commercials, comedy, and burn them onto a compact disc. I would then play each track to the group, ask if they knew what it was, who was playing, singing. Was it from a film or a play? They joined in with enthusiasm, and for an hour or more engaged in enjoying the music, learning more about each piece as we listened and talked about each track.

Eventually the trust responsible for the Day Hospital realized that they didn't have a DBS record check relating to me and they insisted that I go to their office in St Albans to fill out the forms. I had DBS accreditation with the Lister Hospital in order to be a volunteer with the hospital on the same site, but it seemed this wasn't good enough for the trust responsible for mental health.

Off I went to St Albans with all manner of paperwork to prove that I was who I thought I was. I filled out the form as one of their staff closely watched me. Some weeks later, I discovered that they had lost all the paperwork relating to the DBS clearance.

About this time, fourteen years after I had joined as a volunteer, the mental health trust decided it wanted the rooms we used for office space – paperwork before patients – and the group was relocated at a centre operated by a charity called Crossroads. I left the Lister Hospital, having very much enjoyed my time as a volunteer there.

One of the more unusual activities as a volunteer was being asked to role play during examinations for membership of professional medical bodies. This involved a half-day role playing in scenarios designed to test the doctors' ability and skill in certain areas of their professional role. I might be the nephew of a woman admitted to hospital and who had a known allergic reaction to a named drug. On her admission to hospital, I had made sure that the medical team had been informed about this allergy with the plea that she be not given the drug in question. I had returned to hospital the next day to find that this information had been ignored, my aunt had been given the drug provoking a dangerous reaction. What was the doctor going to do about this?

It was a demanding but interesting experience and I estimate that about half of the doctor examinees were failed because of lack of communication skills, or arrogance, doctor-knows-best attitudes and behaviour. I was always asked my opinion by the pairs of examiners after each role play. By the time I had driven home after the session, I was exhausted by the experience. It was heartening though to see that such auditing was in place.

One other activity was for two or three years being a member of the hospital's patient experience committee. In this role, I had a hand in official inspections of parts of the hospital, some involvement in discussions about transition to a different hospital meal regime, discussions about parking problems, patient issues. From time to time I caught myself questioning the whole management approach to such a complex but vital being as the National Health Service, and drawing comparisons with the Church of England's approach to management and leadership, of which I promise more anon.

In the transition from volunteering at the Glaxo Day Hospital to working with Crossroads, I had to have yet another security check for Crossroads to feel secure about me volunteering with them. I also reduced my time from once a week to once a month. I concentrated on the music quiz format at Crossroads, working with some of the original members of the group from the Lister Hospital site. One of them, let's call him Jeff, had an encyclopaedic musical recall, which didn't get any less as he got older in the seventeen years I knew him. He didn't get worse, he just got older. Some patients were with the group for a short period before they needed more intensive care provision. I remember one man who in his professional life had been a neurosurgeon. He liked classical music and so I made a point of including classical music in every quiz when he was present. He recognized each composer's work and would whisper 'Mozart,' 'Beethoven,' or 'Mendelssohn' when

I asked if anyone knew who had composed the piece. He was always right. Dementia is such a cruel disease. But music is one of the best medicines to ease its horror and bring back memories and feelings.

I left the Crossroads volunteer role after about five years when the size of the group shrank to maybe two or three.

One area of volunteering came about when I caught up with my television-repairing fellow student from Lincoln Theological College days, David Matthiae. He retired to live in Duxford with his wife Jill. Early in 1990 I had joined a course in Luton to gain an amateur radio operator's licence. Mercifully it wasn't too difficult as the examiners took into account my previous radio operating licence issued by the Post Office. I had encouraged David to take up amateur radio some years earlier as a break from spending his time being consumed by the Church. He joined the Imperial War Museum at Duxford as a volunteer and between nine and ten years ago he encouraged me to do the same.

Being a volunteer at Duxford is as different from working with dementia sufferers as it could be. The Duxford Radio Society, now called the Duxford Radio Section, has the stewardship of two buildings, 177 and 178 on this World War One airfield alongside the M11 motorway. The buildings contain and display radio equipment old and new, as well as, in Building 177, an amateur radio station from which volunteers who are licensed radio amateurs can talk to operators around the world using microphone or Morse code.

The buildings are between the hangars and the American Air Museum commemorating some 30,000 American aircrew lost or killed while flying from East Anglia during World War Two. Volunteers work 'front of house' meeting members of the public and describing, explaining, or operating some of the equipment. Others toil away repairing equipment, bringing it into use, producing materials and displays which enhance the visitor experience. When children and school parties visit, we demonstrate the Morse code to them and encourage them to try sending their names in code in order to gain a certificate. Since leaving the dementia group, I go to Duxford most Tuesdays, putting in an average of four hours per session.

There has been a shift in how the museum engages with the public. Many more of the exhibits across the site are now interpreted through stories told by those who flew the planes, operated radio and radar sets. These stories are either displayed in print or on video screens. Storytelling seems to be the key.

CHAPTER 19

A sea story or two

While I worked at Church House, Annette and I bought an old twenty-two-foot bilge-keeled motor sailer, *My Girl*. We wanted to explore the Broads after hiring a Broads sailing boat for a week while on holiday. I'm surprised that we weren't put off by that experience.

We had hired the boat from a boatyard at Upton near Potter Heigham. Every other Broads user knows about Potter Heigham, where and when to go under the bridge. A pilot needs to be engaged to move the boat under the bridge. Our boat was a Bermuda sloop with an inboard engine. After about twenty minutes' instruction on how to moor using the mud anchor and how to lower the mast to navigate beneath bridges, off we went, heading for Potter Heigham. In no time at all we had moved under engine beyond the notice which said, 'No further than this without a pilot.' With our mast lowered we were a much longer boat, and it is a wonder that, as we carefully turned around to avoid the bridge and go downstream to somewhere less hazardous, no-one was swept off the quayside by our lowered mast and boom. Just as we thought we had managed to escape, a motor cruiser pulled out from the port bank of the river and I had to throw the engine into full speed astern so as not to collide. We made our way down river exhausted by all this scary excitement and moored using the mud anchor. We altered our plans, having poured a restorative drink or two.

We went ahead and bought the motor-sailer and kept her for about eleven years on a berth in a delightfully friendly marina being developed at Brundall Gardens, just a mile or three downstream of Norwich. My brother Mike looked over the boat and thought it would

My Girl

do. It was designed for the east coast, shallow draught and bilge keels so it could sit on the mud. Its mast was capable of being lowered but we had a clever man make an A-frame so that raising and lowering might be less hazardous. It had a Yanmar single-cylinder diesel engine which seized solid just as we were about to enter Southwold Harbour. A fishing boat rescued us and towed us safely into the river.

We had the engine removed and repaired. It seems that it had been incorrectly installed with the exhaust hose placed at the wrong height which meant that over the years not all the water was vented. We had a diesel tank and a tank to take the toilet waste installed, which improved the boat considerably. I had qualified as an RYA Day Skipper and Coastal Skipper. I had a VHF radio licence, and we used a marine GPS. We kept charts for the areas we were likely to explore, adequate lifejackets and an inflatable, outboard and flares, enough to cope with most emergencies. We could cook on board but liked to explore pubs wherever we tied up.

Over the years we had many enjoyable holidays and some scary voyages. We once approached Southwold and asked for permission

Cabin of My Girl

to enter. The harbour master, or more accurately, harbour mistress, said Southwold was full and we could not enter. As one of the pins supporting the rudder had sheared on the way south from Lowestoft, I replied by declaring an emergency and insisting that we be allowed in. She was probably very cross, although the emergency was genuine, and directed us to the most inaccessible berth seen in the history of that harbour.

Eventually we got older and sailing and keeping a boat became more and expensive. The Broads Authority introduced a controversial boat safety scheme which required all boats on the Broads to be brought up to safety standards, a bonanza for boatyards and engineers. Marine diesel was about to lose its price concession and become much more expensive. We advertised *My Girl* and got two sniffs of interest, one from a Nigerian fraudster, 'We will pay you in cash far more than you are asking, provided you help us launder the money through your accounts.' The other interest was from two splendid Irishmen from Dingle in the southwest of Ireland. They were looking for a boat in which to explore the Shannon and other rivers.

We met them off the plane at Stansted and drove them to Norfolk, stopping at Elveden for coffee on the way to Brundall. They looked all over the boat, paid 10 per cent of the price in cash, took us to lunch in a pub, and said they would pay the balance into our account which they did. We took them back to Bishop's Stortford where they booked into a hotel for the night. All the way to Norfolk and back they talked non-stop about racehorses, their other consuming interest. One of them managed the sightseeing boats which travel from Dingle out into the bay to see Dingle's famous dolphin Fungie.

After my brother Mike retired from the Royal Navy he worked for a while for the John Lewis Partnership. He became one of the Partnership's Yacht Master trainers. On a number of occasions, he offered me berths on some of the Partnership yachts.

Sailing one day off the Normandy coast there was a problem with the boat's VHF set. We thought it could be the masthead aerial fitting, so I was winched up the mast of this ketch, *Sabeema*, in a bosun's chair to sort it out. Of course, at the top of the mast any roll of the yacht is magnified, and I was treated to a very moving picture of the French coast. I sorted out the aerial and was quite glad to be let down from the masthead. One of my treasured photographs is of five of us caught in mid-air jumping into the sea off Normandy. The picture was taken by our sixth crew member who had brought his waterproof camera with him.

One day Mike rang me at Church House and asked if I could get time off to help bring a boat down from Scotland to Barmouth in Wales to take part in the Three Peaks yacht race. I was able to agree to do this and we travelled north to pick up the boat and the runners who would take part in the race. I was on watch in the Irish Sea as we came south at night. My watchman was too busy being sick over the side to be a huge help looking out.

Years earlier while I had been working for St Albans Diocese, the printer responsible for printing the diocesan monthly *See Round* told me he had a yacht and asked if I would like to sail with him from Swanwick Marina near Portsmouth to Alderney in the Channel Islands. Of course, I said yes and off we set, crossing the Channel by night. There were just the two of us aboard. I had the watch as we sailed *Vertuosity* across the channel sea lanes. Michael Taylor popped up to see how we were doing as we approached the northbound shipping lane. He pointed to a merchant ship I had already seen. 'You can cross in front of that one,' he said. 'I don't think so,' I replied. He said, 'Well, you're in charge,' and returned to his bunk. We made it safely to Alderney but left there on a misty morning to return to Swanwick. The mist turned into fog and at one point we heard a very loud ship's siren fine on the port bow. We kept a close eye and ear on this, and at one point the fog lifted to reveal one of the Cunard liners passing a mile or so off our port side.

On a subsequent voyage with Michael Taylor and my brother Mike, we discovered that Michael Taylor was colour blind. He admitted as much as we tried to distinguish the myriad lights as we entered Poole Harbour at night. We didn't sail with him again. Years later I was asked to take his funeral service after he died of cancer.

Brother Mike bought a quarter share in a big Bavaria yacht kept in Split Marina in Croatia. Annette and I had many happy weeks discovering the fabulous Adriatic, the islands offshore, the water temperatures generally around 21 degrees Celsius. We were reminded once or twice about the dangers of relaxing too much as winds can sweep down from the mountains along Croatia's coast and really stir up the Adriatic to anything but pleasant. We once picked up the boat in Montenegro and had to leave port and sail an uncomfortable seven hours till we reached port at Split.

One day Mike asked me to help bring a boat he had skippered from Portugal on its last lap from Dinan to Ouistreham in Normandy. He had been asked to make this voyage by a French teacher who used to sail his boat to Portugal each summer, spend time pottering about and then leave the boat in Portugal for someone else to bring it back to Ouistreham. I flew to Dinan and the next day we left to sail north around the Cherbourg peninsula. It was a beautiful day with a swell running.

It was the swell, alas, that hid a lobster pot float from our view. The mooring line was snagged by the boat's propeller and we were brought up short. The strain on the line and the propeller shaft was worryingly strong. We tried everything to bring the line on board so we could cut it but there was too much tension. Eventually it was decided that with lifejacket and a safety line attached to the boat I should be lowered head-first over the side to find the line and cut it with a Stanley knife. I took a deep breath and with Mike holding onto my ankles I went over the side. It only took me to lay the edge of the blade against the line for the strain to cause it to part.

It was clear that the propeller or the shaft was bent, so we had to sail to Guernsey and enter port at night without the help of the engine. Mike called up a boatyard on the VHF and arranged for the boat to be hauled out of the water the following morning so that the shaft and propeller could be examined.

We left the boat in the yard's hands and enjoyed a pleasant lunch after which we returned to the boatyard to find that the shaft was true but that one blade on the propeller needed bending back into its proper position. We left St Peter Port to resume our voyage to Ouistreham. We travelled along the north coast of the peninsula at night, a watch that I shared with the third member of the crew. Mist descended the next morning as we turned south towards Ouistreham as we strained to see or hear any Brittany Ferries ship coming into Caen from Portsmouth. The boat's owner put us up a bit grumpily, given the costs of our unscheduled stop in Guernsey together with some other engine problems encountered on the way from Portugal.

I looked at the electrical connections on a panel inside the main hatch from the main deck. I found that some were so insecure they were kept in place by broken matches. I think we did well to survive the parlous state of that yacht. I don't think Mike would have agreed to sail her again if he had been asked.

CHAPTER 20

A gathering of elephants

You may have noticed the odd hint or clue about my feelings about the Church of England. This last chapter – take heart – is the moment to look a little more closely into the big question: Is there a future for the Church of England? I hope and I believe there is, but not without massive change, and probably a great deal of pain.

What is the point and purpose of the Church? I don't like the answer, 'To put bums on seats and keep the rumour of God alive.' I much prefer the Thamesmead mission statement: 'To share the gospel of Jesus Christ and to serve the community for its own sake without strings.' I am sure some wordsmith can put that better. On a poster for our church noticeboard I put the slogan, 'Here for God, here for you.' I was in 'few words' mode, just as I was when I tried to put a message from God into a shorter form than the Holy Bible, 'I am God. You are my child. So is Jesus. Listen to him, follow him, find me. Love me with all your heart, mind, soul, and strength, and love my children, your neighbours, as you love yourself. My Spirit will help. That's it. Lots of love, God.' Short and to the point, I hope. So, is the Church of England fit for purpose? In our present state, probably not.

I will start with people. I understand that a recent statistic showed some 7,000 clergy, helped, I hope, by around the same number of allegedly retired clergy. This is nowhere near the number of clergy needed to maintain the myth that everyone in England can look for pastoral care to the Church. And I have immediately fallen into a trap carefully and invisibly built by years of tradition, history, and practice, that of thinking or maybe even believing that ministry is the preserve of the ordained clergy.

Sweeping up after my nephew's wedding in America

If clergy are believed to be suffering from stress in significant numbers, this must be partly due to this heresy about ministry. What ever happened to the phrases 'every member ministry' and the 'priesthood of all believers'? Did anyone ever believe them enough to put them into practice?

Has any social scientist calculated the sheer costs of trying to do all that is required of the Church with just 14,000 clergy, half of whom are supposed to be retired, along with some 8,000 readers or licensed lay ministers? I am told these keep dying off, and are not being replaced in the same number because the powers that be have made the training much too arduous and academic.

We should immediately look at the necessity to get rid of the denominational aspect of church and faith. I see no point now in maintaining all the different denominations, including our own, with their systems, bureaucracies, buildings, procedures, governance, and associated nonsense. The Week of Prayer for Christian Unity needs to become the Campaign for Christian Unity, round the clock and round the year. This is not a move to make us feel stronger as numbers continue to decline. It is a move to strengthen the work of Christ across the land. And if that causes alarm and disquiet, so be it. It will be as nothing when compared to the growing despair at what is passing for church. Jesus prayed that we should all be one. Let's do it.

A few years back, we arranged the celebration of a Roman Catholic Mass in our little village church. It was taken by a neighbouring Roman Catholic parish priest from Biggleswade and was well attended. It was the first such Mass since the Reformation, and there has been another since then, this time taken by the Roman Catholic priest from Baldock, whose parish, in fact, includes our village.

I suspect most Christian denominations are dying the same slow death as is the Church of England. I don't fear death, whether it is of the church I have tried to serve or my own. Week by week I affirm my faith in the resurrection. So I can be clear-eyed about what I see around me, my own certain death, weakening of the body, the failure of memory, and the public will to steal away and do other things on Sundays.

Who needs denominations? Who needs over a hundred types of bread in a supermarket? I believe that what matters more than denominations is the number of people strong enough to say they are Christians in a puzzling world. What must the different churches, denominations, sects, expressions fresh or stale, spend each day to maintain their separateness? Jesus prayed that his followers might be one. Maybe we haven't been praying hard enough for his prayer to be answered. Yet an enormous amount of energy, time, and money is shelled out to avoid that one-ness.

So rather than devise strategies to save the life of the Church of England, I suggest that a more challenging question is the unity of those who claim to be Christian. For some thirteen years in St Albans, I was a member of the Board for Mission and Unity. To be honest,

I remember few if any debates about either. I referred earlier to my experience fifty years ago of the Week of Prayer for Christian Unity in Yeovil, and my concern about the myriad of churches and chapels competing for attention, membership, funds. Praying for unity for 2 per cent of the year is not enough. I got into trouble writing about that then. The challenge is so much more urgent now.

Christian unity matters not just because Jesus prayed for it but because divisions among people of faith eat away at what can be done, willed and achieved. The Church of England is nearly famous for the breadth of its belief and membership. It is only when we go through the agonies of debating whether women may be ordained, made bishops, whether same sex marriage or partnerships may be celebrated and affirmed, that we discover just how corrosive breadth of opinions and deeply held enmities can be.

I don't believe unity, if it ever comes and I pray that it will, will happen by institutional edict from above. If people in parishes and districts really want it, it can begin now, it can start here, if it hasn't already. I didn't ask my bishop if it would be possible for a Roman Catholic priest to celebrate the first Mass since the Reformation in our little church, which centuries ago was his church. There are Roman Catholics living in this village and they had been more than generous in delivering letters I had written about raising money to fund an oak building in which there would be a meeting room, kitchen, and toilet on the church site. Great Offley welcomed a monthly Roman Catholic Mass in the late 1960s. In 1969 Thamesmead was an ecumenical project before the first residents moved in.

I dream of the end of denominational nonsense and the growth of Christian communities and groups where allegiance to one or another historical branch of church matters less than a commitment to being Christian wherever God puts us. When we came to Hinxworth, I was delighted to discover we had a Methodist organist, a Roman Catholic churchwarden and, eventually, a Baptist lay pastor in the congregation. Isn't that part of the way forward?

Church leaders and lawyers might choke on their muesli – let them if they must. Anyway, they haven't time or cause to be indignant, they have work to do. One bishop I remember claimed that he was a symbol of unity and tried to demonstrate it by walking down a high street in a local town one day hand in hand with his Roman Catholic episcopal colleague. I believe Church leaders, visionaries all I trust, need to invest time, energy, thought, and prayer in getting to know their colleagues of other faiths. For the divide in our society is not now, if it ever was, between Anglicans and Roman Catholics but between people of faith and those of no faith. I go back to the plea in *Priestland's Progress* by Bishop Michael Hare Duke, 'to find the Spirit of God in other world religions, make contact with them, and not tell them to forget the lot and start again.'

So let Christians at the local level begin to learn of their unity, perhaps despite their history or possibly because of it, and forge new ways of being Christian together the year round, while their elders and maybe betters get on with discovering true bonds of faith and love with their colleagues from other faiths.

One of the joys of working in local radio religious broadcasting was discovering, as the Quakers might put it, 'God in everyone.' Secure in our relationships of Baptists, Methodists, Anglicans, Roman Catholics within the production team, we enjoyed the security and confidence to explore the riches and delights of other faith traditions within our audience area. I have written that this didn't necessarily meet with approval from members of Anglican deanery synods, who would rather we used religious broadcasting to do their evangelism for them.

How much of what we do is religious, and how much is faith-full? There's a question for the theologians and teachers of the Church. I find religion, the thoughtless obeying of rules and regulations, the list of deeds approved or forbidden, to be something of a killer. I suspect Jesus did, does, too. Faith is what challenges me, encourages me, keeps me going and gives me love and joy and laughter.

Did I sleep through seminars on canon law while at theological college? Can I get excited by an A3 laminated sheet of what may or may not be allowed to happen in an Anglican churchyard? Probably not as it would take someone with better eyesight than mine to be able to read the tiny print. Maybe Lincoln Theological College led the way in not worrying our student heads about such things, in which case I thank God.

Clearly among the characteristics that put people off the church are the attitudes and behaviour of the clergy. 'He is far too smells-and-bells for me, she is too clappy-happy for me. He seems preoccupied with sin and guilt, while she can't stop smiling.' And so it goes. Perhaps a recovery of the notion of every member ministry, supposing it ever existed, might make a dent in the influence for ill that some of us appear to wield. I have heard people complain of a culture of clericalism among clergy where more importance seems to attach to language, clothing, impression, and attitude than to the guts of the gospel. I could imagine howls of rage from ecclesiastical outfitters if we became less thrilled about cassocks, cottas, lappets, preaching gowns, bands, and copes. The way things are, the last thing we need is more clergy, so problematic is their care, their status, their point and purpose. What we need are millions of committed Christians, lay or ordained.

Given how long and difficult it proved to agree to the ordination of women first as priests and then as bishops, and the lengthy debate about sexuality and what this priest or that minister may be doing in their bedroom, the question of 'every member ministry' as a principle could be years and years away. We have not got years and years; the need is now. 'Setting God's People Free' must not be about training, examinations, licensing, but about a true freeing of people from all manner of nonsense to be the people God is calling us to be. The Church of England discusses reform and renewal. I think that is a spelling mistake. We must be about revolution.

For those clergy who remain, their movement from post to post needs to be simplified. The whole process of managing vacancies is fraught with elephant traps. Questions about parish profiles, when an advertisement can be placed, and what it may say needs sorting. Yes, there are legal questions but there seem to be major problems – the chronic shortage of ordained priests, the ponderous process of consulting patrons and their advice or permission. What can other churches teach us about the movement of clergy? To place a single advertisement in a church newspaper can set back a parish's finances by hundreds of pounds. If 'every-member ministry' was a reality or objective agreed by the Church of England, vacancies should become less of a challenge. I know, it's a big if.

Vacancies can last anything from a few months to a few years, leaving parishioners to do what they can to ensure services are taken, weddings taken, funerals held with all the accompanying pastoral visiting. I heard one bishop complain that the parishes in his diocese fondly imagined that he had any number of spare clergy available which he kept in a large cupboard ready to deploy as required. I have also observed that some dioceses will export people they would never again appoint to a parish, to a less-suspecting bishop or diocese in the hope that they will never again see said priest in their diocese. I am told that an archdeacon refers to this practice as 'throwing dead cats over the wall.'

Vacancies are not all bad. It is possible for all kinds of good things to happen when there is no priest in post. A good priest will encourage all manner of creativity and make a point of celebrating the gifts and talents of members of the congregations, and vacancies could be an opportunity for these gifts and talents to be given full rein. Where, however, parishioners have become dependent on having a priest, the easy option is for them to bewail the lack of their own priest and complain about everything and everyone. If denominational differences were to melt away, as I pray they might, then vacancies could be more easily handled. We could all go to the United Reformed, or the Methodist, or any other formerly 'competing' building and they could come to be with us.

When we were first at Hinxworth, during a vacancy, I managed to cope with maybe two services on Sunday, funerals, weddings, the occasional baptism, and all the visiting required for these events. Now in my eighty-third year, I view the fifth vacancy due to start in October this year, with some foreboding. Lately I have found that preparing and taking large village funerals reduces me to a cross between pulp and a dangerous jelly. Funerals just must be right and absolutely the very best one can do. The odd glitch at a wedding will generally be forgiven, funerals not so much if at all. I have shared this apprehension with our parish priest, and he has kindly understood, letting me be involved but without the stress of overseeing the service. When he retires because he will be seventy years old, I will just have to see what I can usefully contribute without further setting back the course of Christianity in this place. I recently read that the Church of England's oldest priest had retired in his nineties. Well done, him. May he enjoy a long and joyful retirement.

One truth I think I have discovered is that this united benefice with a smallish population is not a pushover ideal for a first-time incumbency appointment, as the last archdeacon believed and stated publicly at a meeting of members of all the parishes during the last vacancy. I wrote to him a day or two after the meeting and asked if that is what he had said or was I having a nightmare. If he had said that, I wrote, I thought he was profoundly wrong, and then went on to enumerate the reasons.

Bless him, he wrote back to say that on reflection he was wrong, and I was right. Happily, the appointment that followed was of someone who had been ordained some twenty-five years earlier, had successfully run a business, had been a rural dean, worked in rural parishes, and had a considerable degree of experience. The difference that this has made to the benefice has been massive and good. I have been in touch with that archdeacon's successor to try to ensure that the lesson may have been learned before the next appointment is made. I have also written in the same terms to the bishop who will be involved with the process.

People, ministry, what else? How about money? It was many years before I discovered that I was not employed by the Church of England. I could have worked this out as I read in the late 1960s news stories of clergy trying to take the Church to employment tribunals. The Church said, 'You are not employed, so you have no rights to hearings before employment tribunals. If anyone is your employer, it may be God.' It seems that while I was a priest working for the Church of England, I was an officeholder which, I guess, meant that I had few if any rights to do with stipends, terms of employment, working conditions, housing. I read somewhere that I was paid a stipend precisely in order that I did not have to work, so that I would be able to fulfil my ministry.

The Church of England has immense wealth; it is one of England's largest landowners. The Church Commissioners administer funds worth around £8.3 billion to support the life and work of the Church. If the Church worked with other denominations, disposed of many duplicated buildings, who knows how much wealth might be available for the real work of the Church?

As I write this closing chapter on St Patrick's Day, 17 March 2020, the Archbishops of Canterbury and York have written to their clergy calling for churches to put public worship on hold and become a different sort of church in the coming months to face the challenge of coronavirus. I warm to the idea of a different sort of church.

Let's look at where we are. We are the people of God, whatever that means. We are the people who believe in Jesus who died on a cross and came back from the dead on the third day. As a result, everything is changed, anything is possible. We are all children of God, you too even if you don't believe it. We are a broad church, the Church of England. We won't limit you to believing as few as six impossible things before breakfast. When we use words, they mean just what we choose them to mean, neither more nor less, as Humpty Dumpty might have said in a rather scornful tone. And when we can't find the right word we may, like professionals in other lines of work, hide behind a word which only we can understand, be it ecclesiastical jargon, New Testament Greek, or Aramaic on a really bad day.

We are notionally pastorally responsible for everyone who lives in England, for that is the country in which our Church of England is established. Our clergy, probably the majority, are registrars for the state, and so can conduct weddings whose validity is accepted by the state, provided they are not sham weddings conducted by naughty vicars in order to make money to supplement their stipends.

We have made things too complicated, allowed too much to be added to the picture. I imagine the first friends of Jesus would have a terrible problem trying to make any kind of sense of it at all. Eliza Doolittle in Lerner and Loewe's *My Fair Lady* sings 'Don't talk of love, show me!' and the more the church turns the Son of God, the Word made flesh, back into words, the more I think Eliza Doolittle got it absolutely right. As the poster observes, God didn't send a committee, he sent his Son.

At Thamesmead, we discussed one day what we did think the Church was for. Looking back, Jim Thompson, rector of Thamesmead said, 'We decided we would get totally stuck into the community, that it wasn't just about an ecumenical group, which we were, it wasn't just winning new converts, but it was also about trying to convert the community so that it would be a place where human beings would flourish. We had two aims, one of which was to share the gospel of Jesus Christ; the other was to serve the community, without strings attached.' In his book *A Future That's Bigger Than the Past*, Samuel Wells, vicar of St Martin in the Fields, writes of ways in which the Church can become a blessing to both the community it serves and the those who are members. His is a book I read from end to end and wholeheartedly commend to anyone who clings to hope for the Church and wonders how to move forward. I have not tinkered with Jim Thompson's words but would suggest, 'share the gospel of Jesus Christ, serve the community without strings and become a blessing.'

This seemed to us to be a useful approach to being church. It can be the means by which people can discover that, perhaps contrary to their worst fears and nightmares, they are valued, loved, died for. I want to be part of a church that serves people in a foot-washing way, is prepared to get down and dirty where the needs are, a church with, as the report Faith in the City put it, 'a bias to the poor,' who, you will have noticed, are always with us. I believe that is what we attempted at Thamesmead.

Just suppose for a mad moment that the point and purpose of the Church is indeed to tell people about God and Jesus, and serve them for their own sake without strings, and become a blessing, what have I learned that might identify the many elephants in the Church's rooms and begin to make some suggestions about changing the Church?

A large elephant in the room is the matter of buildings. When Annette and I went to Offley and Lilley, I don't think either of us had a clue about the state of disrepair of St Mary Magdalene Church. Had we known the amount of money that would need to be raised to bring it into a safe condition, would we have moved there? We certainly did not know of the complications of English Heritage being involved, who, regardless of the resources available, might err on the side of insisting that only particularly expensive methods or materials be used in any remedial works.

Yes, a well-maintained medieval church, whose walls are soaked through with prayer rather than damp, which is used regularly, and which will not threaten to bankrupt its users may well sing the glory of God. But the Church of England must not be sidetracked from putting its prime energies, such as they are, into building up groups of people to stand for God and serving the community for its own sake without strings. Anything, anything which impedes the point and purpose of the Church must be let go.

Where a decision is made to keep a building, it must be made easier to maintain and update it. There are societies set up to keep safe the glories of Georgian and Victorian churches. Perhaps they should be given the very best of such exemplars and encouraged to get on with doing so. It should be possible to make ecumenical cooperation and provision a mandatory question when discussing or deciding the future of our church buildings so that the best buildings are put to work for all Christians and, who knows, people of other faiths too in each place.

At Thamesmead it was five years or so before we built the shared Church of the Cross in Lensbury Way. The decision to go ahead and build was only narrowly won. We had almost grown used to meeting for worship on Sundays in community clubrooms, though the smells from licensed premises on a Sunday morning weren't too helpful. We concluded after much discussion that we did need a building base from which to work, and we decided almost reluctantly to move ahead. But we insisted that the building should serve the community round the week and round the clock.

If such ecumenical co-operation was possible and, in my view, successful all those years ago, what progress has the Church made with buildings and with shared ministry since? Some four years after we left Thamesmead, the *Times* published an article by Roger Suddards, 'Do the empty churches a service – knock them down,' in which he posed the question of what to do with the buildings for which the Church is responsible, while acknowledging just how great a challenge finding an answer might be.

Cartoon character Egbert Nosh found to his surprise that his house was following him on one of his daily walks. The Church has some sixteen thousand buildings, over ten thousand of them medieval, for which it is ultimately responsible. They may not follow their diminishing worshippers around, but their presence may be lifting the hearts of some while bringing nightmares and violent feelings to those who are legally responsible for their preservation and use. I doubt that bright-eyed ordinands spend too much time thinking about the use of buildings until they are ordained by which time it is too late to run away. Is the church a society for the preservation of old buildings? Discuss.

Buildings remain secondary to the aims and objectives, the very purpose and point of the Church. Without some shared agreement about the future of the institution itself, debates about buildings remain a powerful and expensive waste of time.

Remembering Jim Thompson's announcement of rationing me to one idea per year, I would suggest a simple first step for the Church, for the churches, for the denominations. Find no more than a dozen of the most creative thinkers, pay for their accommodation and food, and set them the task of deciding and describing the future of Christianity in the United Kingdom. Or if that treads on too many national church toes, limit it to the Church of England in England.

I have all manner of questions for this group. What is the point and purpose of bishops? How can we rediscover the 'priesthood of all believers' and 'every-member ministry' and how might that impact on the very precious but maybe not entirely essential notion of ordination? What about busting a gut to get people to belong to congregations and then busting other guts to get them out from churches to where all the non-belonging people are and where some might think the real business of the Church could be? Should pensions for clergy be the same whether one retired as an archdeacon or bishop or as a faithful parish priest?

How might the Church be led, governed, from death to life? I read the other day 'Fresh life can come from the compost of Christendom. I think we are poised for another great wakening' (Richard Rohr, 1 January 2020). That chimes with my St George's House Windsor picture of the Church as a compost heap. God is not dead, but the Church is seen as dying on its feet. Why should this worry us if we believe in resurrection? I heard of a bishop who said that his task was to manage the decline of the Church. I don't think bishops are there to manage anything or anyone. They just could be there to be visionary leaders. Managers may well have their place in the day-to-day administration of the ever-burgeoning Church bureaucracy. It really should never have taken six months to find me a desk and a place in which to work. Nor should it take forty-seven pages in a House of Bishops paper to cope with the administration of 'permission to officiate.' And is stealth a gospel way to get objectives achieved? Are there too many dioceses?

For what and for whom is training? How can training be better? Ask some seasoned clergy how much they were helped in their ministry by the training that happened once and may have been topped up since. Just how valuable is theology and those who study it, teach it, use it? The very first Christians probably knew more about fishing than academic or any other kind of theology.

Should care of Christians, church members, lay, and ordained not be a top priority for church leaders? Is seeing a minister once or twice a year adequate pastoral care? I imagine that the question of post-holding versus employment, housing of clergy, maintenance and usefulness of inherited buildings will need to be discussed in the light of agreed conclusions about the point and purpose of the Church of England. As will whether synodical government can be said or seen to be working. And even if it is working, what does that mean, what could that mean? More regulations, endless debates, and mountains of emails? And something must be done about the Clergy Discipline Measure which is driving those accused to suicidal thoughts and attempts.

These are just a few of the questions that the brainstorming group examining the state and life or death of the Church of England need to face. Meanwhile, after over fifty-three years since I was ordained deacon in the Church of God, I wonder whether denominations, including the Church of England, might not be edging towards an accidental death when a planned death and hoped for resurrection might be a more positive outcome.

I suspect that the man and woman in the street in need of care, encouragement, and ministry care little whether these are offered by Anglican, Methodist, Baptist, Roman Catholic, United Reformed, Assemblies of God. What they might want to know is whether it is Sikh, Muslim, Christian, Jewish, or maybe they will just be glad if it is offered at all and is good. I don't believe too many will worry about what the minister's sexual orientation might be, about which the Church of England has seemed most exercised. It is as if a homeless man on being offered accommodation worries about who manufactured the pillow or duvet provided.

However, should the mad ideas group be constituted, I wish them well and look forward to praying for them and their gargantuan and important task. When they have sorted out the Christian content of their discussions, maybe they could spend some time relaxing into a discussion about relationships with other great religions or faith bodies. Tuition in elephant recognition will probably be unnecessary. The elephants are stirring in so many rooms, they should be more than visible by now. Look out, there goes another pachyderm. Unlike their cousins in Africa, our elephants are not in danger of extinction.

This has been a foolish endeavour. Those who know me would have expected nothing less, and I am sorry if they expected very much more. Fools matter, as I have argued elsewhere. Fools are truth tellers, tellers of tall tales with much meaning. I have heard it argued that in its best moments, the Church might be society's fool, prepared to journey day by day but with the calling to say to society, 'This is how it is: if you do this, that will happen as sure as eggs is eggs.' In the 1980s, the Church of England almost took on this role when it published *Faith in the City*, and when it dared to suggest prayers be offered for those who died on both sides in the Falklands conflict. Looking back, the good old Church of England was seen by some as Her Majesty's loyal if unofficial opposition. That was then, this is now. Time for courage, joyful storytelling, the dreaming and realization of impossible but possible dreams.

In this first fifty years or so of being ordained, I have been puzzled, challenged, disturbed by the Church. But despite or perhaps because of the Church, I affirm that it has been, and often remains, a journey packed with challenge and interest and possibilities. The Church, often mistaken for a sort of woolly mammoth, the breadth of belief, and on good days the refusal to take refuge in a wanton misinterpretation of either God or history, to hide inside clericalism, has been an encouragement. A willingness to improvise while set about with probably far too many rules and regulations has been much appreciated. The care I have received along the way has been in the main from family, friends, and colleagues rather than from the institution I try to serve.

Some few things disturb me, the growth of the centre when I have been accustomed to see the edge where life blossoms. The outsourcing of diocesan activities, communications, booking on free conferences seems to me to be plain silly. Will it get to the point when contemplating an evening visit to a spinster living on her own, I need to book a Group 4 or Serco chaperone to make sure I don't abuse or suffer abuse? So far, I have sat through some nine hours of safeguarding training, aware of little but the sounds of stable doors closing and hooves clattering away towards the horizon.

But there remain God, his church and his kingdom, good people, prayers, friends and joy, family and laughter, a trombone yearning to be played, faith, hope, and love, for which an infinity of thanks to all.

AN AFTERWORD

I finished writing this book on St Patrick's Day 2020, shortly before the first pandemic lockdown in this country. It would be silly not to reflect for a minute or two on how the Church has performed when churches have been closed to worship and contact with others has been much reduced and scrutinised subject to the laws of the land.

Services of worship and occasions of virtual meeting have gone online and a large number of people have enjoyed or endured steep learning curves getting to grips with the technology. I find Zoom a great tool but it's not a technology I enjoy. We have had Communion services, meetings of the clergy chapter on Zoom, and clearly they are better than nothing, but not ideal. Some have said, 'Can we have them when we get back to normal?' and I wonder whether this is because it's easier to sit in front of a computer than stir out to a real church service.

While all this has been going on, there are moves afoot to make sense of the Church, in the light of a shortfall in the churches' pension fund, a considerable drop in church income due to churches being closed, to the point where a bishop has gone on record saying that there is no plot to abolish the parish system.

It will be tragic if decisions are made solely because of the effects of the pandemic. I believe that profound thought must be given to the point and purpose of what we think we are about, and only then move on to how this could all be done better.

Perhaps the image that will stay with me will be that of a parish priest in tears as he sees the depths of poverty and suffering which the pandemic has exposed. It needs to be retrieved as a still from the television news and then used perhaps with a cross and a candle to help focus the debates that must follow, and which I hope will begin in depth and in humility.

1 December 2020

ACKNOWLEDGMENTS

I thank friends for their patience and encouragement, especially Chris and Christina Rees. I thank Kirsty Anderson for her editing skills and the Bauhan Publishing crew – Sarah Bauhan, Mary Ann Faughnan, and Henry James – for their publishing expertise. I hope Mary Young, whose painting inspires the front cover, enjoys the elephants so skillfully added by illustrator Alison Gates. I am grateful beyond measure to colleagues who have inspired me to continue the journey.

PICTURE CREDITS

All photos except the ones listed below are from the author. We have done our best to find and credit the photographers, but in the case of the frontispiece and the photo of the pantomime horse on Lambeth Bridge on page 173, we weren't successful. Both those photos were taken by freelance photographers working for the *Times.*

Page 11: Roly Bain and Me, © Rachel Morton, used by permission

Page 24: The *Northern Spray,* ©Jim Porter, *Bosun's Watch,* used by permission

Page 27: The London Telegraph Training College, ©Grace's Guide to British Industrial History, used by permission

Page 31: RMS *Loch Gowan* ©Fotoflite, used by permission

Page 33: MV *Sugar Importer* ©Fotoflite, used by permission

Page 52: Lincoln Theological College by Richard Croft. Licensed under the Creative Commons Attributions-share alike Generic license.

Page 124: St Peter's Lilley, ©Hugh J Griffiths, eimagesite.net, used by permission

Page 131: St Peter's Lilley, ©Hugh J Griffiths, eimagesite.net, used by permission

Page 187: Pantomime Horse. ©Missions to Seafarers, used by permission